It's All
GRACE

Kimberly Nilsson

It's All
GRACE

Surviving My Husband's Suicide
to Sparkling Like a Sapphire
in the Sun

Kimberly Nilsson

DEDICATION

My late husband, Nils, was an extraordinary man. He left his mark all over the world during his short but full forty-nine years. Nils touched the lives of so many through his travels and work. He was a beacon of light, and he continues to be. He inspired so many others to think big for the sheer joy of it. He was a force to be reckoned with. The way he died is not a reflection of the enormous love he had for his family, his friends, and life itself. Nils's suicide was both tragic and reformative. I look forward to reconnecting with my beloved Nils in one of the parallel universes he so believed in. As we told each other, "I love you more today than yesterday."

I dedicate this book to everyone who has lost a loved one to suicide or addiction, to those who have attempted suicide, to all our brothers and sisters who have completed suicide, and to those suffering from mental health issues or drug and alcohol addictions.

This book is also dedicated to freely expressing oneself. There is always hope. There is light in the dark. We are *all* in this together.

Paperback ISBN 978-1-960090-77-5
eBook ISBN 978-1-960090-80-5

Library of Congress Control No. 2024913122
Book and cover design by Lisa Carta Design
Cover photo: View of the top of Mont Blanc du Tacul,
Art4401 | Wikimedia Commons
Photo page 20: Edwardje | Dreamstime.com
Author photo by Mary Curran Hackett

Epigraph Books
22 East Market Street, Suite 304
Rhinebeck, New York 12572
845-876-4861

Visit https://www.kimberlynilsson.com

CONTENTS

DISCLAIMER

The contents of this book are for informational purposes only and are not a substitute for professional medical advice, diagnosis, or treatment. The author's intent is only to tell her personal story and to offer information of a general nature to help you in your quest for emotional, physical, and spiritual well-being. Neither the author nor the publisher is responsible for any adverse effects resulting from your use of or reliance on any information contained in this book. Some of the names in *It's All Grace* have been changed to protect individuals' privacy.

IF YOU ARE IN CRISIS

If you are in crisis or think you may have an emergency, call your doctor or 988 (Suicide and Crisis Lifeline) immediately. If you are having suicidal thoughts or other mental health issues, or are struggling with addiction, call 988 at any time, day or night, to talk to a skilled, trained counselor. If you are outside the United States, call your local emergency line immediately.

I can't assuage your pain with any words, nor should I. . . .

And it must burn its purifying way to completion.

For something in you dies when you bear the

unbearable, and it is only in that dark night

of the soul that you are prepared to

see as God sees, and to

love as God loves.

RAM DASS

FOREWORD

My first husband and the father of my daughter died by suicide when she was a teenager..... This I know from our family's experience: Losing someone we love to suicide is unbearable. I understand this journey deeply and the need we all have for support and inspiration in the midst of unspeakable pain. In *It's All Grace*, Kimberly chronicles her journey from the shock and horror of her beloved husband Nils's suicide to the radiant grace, sobriety, and sparkle in her life today.

With the help of friends, 12-step program, meditation, and prayer, Kimberly gradually healed from the cascading losses of Nils's children, parents, and their loving life together. Her determination to seek absolution from the guilt of not being able to prevent Nils's death led her to bravely seek out and explore sources of forgiveness, friendship, and community. Her willingness to write honestly about being lost in layers of misfortune, rage and despair can inspire you, too, to trust that you can recover from heartbreak and shame. Whether or not you have lost a loved one to suicide or addiction, whatever your suffering may be, *It's All Grace* is a trustworthy guide to recovery and healing. Reading this book is like having a friend's kind hand to hold through your hardest times—a friend who offers this comforting wisdom: even the agony of grief can transform into a new life of gratitude and freedom.

Kimberly's compassionate generosity shines through *It's All Grace* as well as the courage that helped her persist in staying sober and embark on new pathways to free her heart from the "if-only's" that torment survivors. When Kimberly places Nils's photo in the holy Ganges

River with infinite tenderness, she reminds all of us that love never diminishes and that, mercifully, we do not have to move on. Even when love seems lost forever, it's possible to find ways to honor and celebrate what once was and be open to loving again.

It's All Grace invites us to wear life like a loose garment where all that matters is our care for one another and this miraculous world. Kimberly leaves us all with a simple question: what would love have you do today?

Read this book slowly and let it touch your heart; meditate with it, reflect and let it hold your hand. Let it help you find your own way through loss and sorrow to the beauty of timeless love and sparkling being.

Trudy Goodman, PhD
Founder of InsightLA,
Cofounder of the Institute for Meditation and Psychotherapy
July 2024

INTRODUCTION

When I stepped onto the five-gallon bucket in our carport, I didn't want to kill myself. Still, I put our dog's leash over the rafter and wrapped it around my neck. I wasn't sure I wanted to live either. What I did know was that I wanted to be close to my husband, Nils, my love and my best friend. I wanted to be connected to him in a visceral, tangible way.

He'd been gone for over a month. I say *gone* as though he were away on a business trip to New York, Moscow, or St. Petersburg, Russia, but he wouldn't be traveling for business anymore. He wasn't telemark skiing on Mont Blanc either, or out on a run near our home in Collonge-Bellerive, Switzerland. Nor was he playing table tennis with his four beautiful children. He wasn't doing any of the things that he—a man of adventure and passion—loved to do. I still was able to convince myself, though (well, for a moment or two), that he was away doing one of these things, hoping that what had happened was a terrible dream and I would wake up.

But it wasn't a dream. It was a living, breathing nightmare from the moment on May 8, 2011, that Nils walked into the carport of our home, stepped up on that five-gallon bucket, looped our dog's leash over the rafter and then around his neck, stepped off the bucket, and ended his earthly life—and our life together. The reality was suicide and its aftermath. And since the unbearable moment that I discovered his near-lifeless body hanging, followed by the gut-wrenching days I sat beside him in the hospital as he clung to life support, everything I thought I knew—about Nils, life, God, and myself—was turned upside down. I was adrift like the boy in the story *Life of Pi* who suddenly finds himself alone on a tiny lifeboat in the ocean and has to fend for himself, all the while feeling abandoned by God. Pi learned to live with imaginal and actual beasts, to conquer his fears, and ultimately, to find his way home.

I was in no mood to be reminded of any of this. *I had a home. I had a husband. I had a life I cherished,* and I wanted them all back. I wanted Nils back! I wanted the ache in my heart to go away. More than anything, I wanted him to take me in his arms, wrap me inside them as he had countless times before, and tell me he would take care of everything. But that was not going to happen. That was never going to happen again.

✳   ✳   ✳

Grieving a suicide can be complex and traumatic. In most parts of the world, suicide is still wrapped in shame. Since the worldwide pandemic of 2020–2023, mental health issues like depression are being discussed more openly among public figures, and people have even begun speaking of suicide a little more openly, although many still whisper and look for other causes to explain a death. When someone dies of a disease, we blame the disease and raise money to defeat it. When someone dies from gun violence, we might pour our energies into gun control. When someone gets hit by a drunken driver, there's a focus for our anger. But when a loved one chooses to leave us, or so it seems, all emotions suffocate us at once. We scream. We blame. We bargain. We cry.

In the days following Nils's death, I coursed through many of the stages of grief described by Elisabeth Kübler-Ross in her classic book, *On Death and Dying.* One minute I was in denial, the next anger, the following minute bargaining with God, and then suddenly overcome by loneliness. I felt disembodied, as if I'd have a psychotic break and never return to myself.

What grounded me was the notion I could *find* Nils—find a way to be near him. I was that desperate to connect with him. Some of his friends and family claimed they could "feel" his presence. I didn't, at least not the Nils I had known. That's the one I wanted back, the one I wanted to touch and be near. And I tried doing that in the carport.

The carport had been a happy place for us. We never used it for cars, but instead for sports equipment and workouts. We lived in a large home in a village on the left bank of Lake Geneva, fifteen minutes from the center of Geneva, Switzerland. There were horse stables down the road and farms not far away, which made the area special. Our neighbor had a rooster fondly known as "our alarm clock." During fall and winter, we could see beautiful Lake Geneva, and in spring and summer, there were bodacious trees to admire. The kids lived with us two weeks per month.

We kept the Ping-Pong table in the carport, too, and would pull it onto the driveway when we wanted to play. The kids stored their bikes and scooters there. Nils taught his son, Charlie, to use the pull-up bar there, and he dangled a punching bag from one of the rafters and used it to de-stress and center himself. On occasion, his oldest daughters, Emma and Mia, would also use the punching bag, while the little ones, Clara and Charlie, ran into it to make it swirl. The little ones pretended to work out too and would sit on their dad's back while he was doing push-ups and would giggle like crazy.

The carport represented our lives: fun, active, adventuresome, and communal. It was attached to the guesthouse, where Nils had his office. We were in and out of the carport every day, but after Nils died, I avoided it. When the little ones wanted to play table tennis, I'd go in quickly and set the table up in the driveway. I even avoided looking at the carport, pretending it no longer existed.

Only Oliver, our Welsh Terrier, wanted to be there. One day I found him curled up in a ball in the exact spot I'd found Nils, as if he sensed energetically the last place Nils had been on earth. Like me, Oliver was looking for his friend. And like me, Oliver was looking to spend a few more moments with Nils. After finding Oliver there on a regular basis, I started to bring fresh flowers to the space—for Oliver, Nils, and me.

In this small way, I tried to reclaim the space that had been a source of such happiness for our family. I *knew* that if I could make peace with the place Nils had ended his life, I could make peace in any situation. So, Oliver and I would often lie there together talking to Nils, telling him how much we missed him, how much we loved him, how much he meant to us, and how sorry we were that he was in such deep darkness that he felt suicide was his only option.

Joan Didion called it *magical thinking.* I wanted to believe I could be near Nils again, that none of what had happened was real. I felt that if I just *followed* the steps he took on the day of his suicide, I could be with him, I could connect with him. And so, one day I did just that.

I started in his office, imagining that was where he had made the decision that would change so many lives. Since then, I've learned his office was indeed where he made his last few phone calls and who he spoke with last. I've learned about the pressure he was under from some of his business dealings. And I learned that the toxicology report confirmed cocaine was in his system. Standing in his office, I imagined his self-loathing, his discomfort, and the powerlessness he must have been feeling—and choosing to handle it all on his own.

Then I began to beat myself up. *What if I hadn't gone to my 12-step meeting that Sunday morning? What if I had left him a note reminding him how much I loved him? Did he doubt my love for even a second? How could he?* That question would play on a loop: *How could he not know how much I loved him? How much I needed him? How could he not know how much his kids loved and adored him? How could he not knowhowdevastatinghisdeathwouldbe?Howcouldheleaveus?* I wanted— I needed—to know.

His office was adorned with the kids' drawings, math equations on the chalkboard, happy family pictures, and abounding signs of life and love. I looked at everything as he might have seen it one last time and walked out the door of the guesthouse, across the driveway, onto the long walkway to the front entry gate, then opened the mailbox and grabbed a leash. Then I went back up the walkway and across the driveway to the spot in the carport where Nils had hung himself. I took every step deliberately, hoping desperately to *feel* him, hoping he would come out from wherever he was hiding and stop me.

When I got to the carport, I grabbed the bucket while holding on to the leash. I pushed the bucket beneath the rafter just as he must have done. Then I stood on it, looped the leash over the rafter and around my neck. For a solitary moment I thought, *I can do this. I can end my suffering right now. It could all be over.* And suddenly, I understood: *This is what Nils must have felt.* Standing on the bucket, he must have felt that the pain was too much to bear, that it could be over in a second, and that his family and friends would be better off without him. This seems to be a common theme among those who have survived suicide attempts. Who could blame Nils for wanting such agony to end? *I wanted it to end, too!* And then another wave of knowing came over me—followed by a sense of calm. *One small move and this bucket could tip over, and I could die*, followed by *We are all going to die, so why not now?*

But I very much wanted to live. I wanted to live for Nils. I wanted to live for us. And then another strong feeling arose that, in the end, Nils wanted that, too. And I sensed, intensely, that as Nils stepped off the bucket, he didn't want to die. I had a flashback, almost a vision, that Nils tried to correct himself and stop it, but it was too late. I knew on a deep level that Nils would never intentionally inflict suffering on anyone he cared for but that he was incapable in those final moments of comprehending the mountains of grief that would be created by this action. He simply wanted his own suffering to stop, which, like most of our suffering, is created in our minds. I took the leash off my neck, stepped down from the bucket, and spent the rest of the day in the carport sitting with Oliver. Overwhelmed with grief, I cried and cried and cried.

And then I felt something else: that during the cocaine crash, he was likely overcome by guilt and shame, that he was a disappointment to his family and those he respected. He had put his and his daughter's lives in danger the night before he took his life. He was ashamed that he'd relapsed, was struggling with getting sober again, and tried to convince himself it wasn't a big deal. On a couple of occasions, he'd told me that he sometimes felt inadequate as a person and a father and that becoming successful in business had helped compensate for not feeling good enough, even though others experienced him as dynamic and extremely confident. Several months before his death, Nils discovered that a business associate he'd trusted had deceived him, which created financial challenges but even more deeply impacted him on a personal level. He also shared about a very personal choice he'd made years earlier and asked me to uphold his privacy. I encouraged him to embrace his choice and to be open about it, but he refused. Using cocaine or other substances can amplify unresolved issues.

Nils was a sensitive person who wanted the love and respect of those around him. His family loved him deeply and was so proud of all of his accomplishments. His business associates also admired his creativity, hard work, and intelligence. He was learning to love himself and to take in all the love soulfully that I and others felt for him. I often reminded him how beautiful he was, both inside and out. He was vulnerable with me and needed encouragement. As an addiction specialist and a recovering addict myself, I know intimately how challenging it can be to get sober and how straightforward it is to stay sober. I also know how serious comedowns from cocaine can be, how they increase the likelihood of self-harm and grip an otherwise reasonable mind. But I never believed Nils was capable of killing himself. And Nils never thought a relapse would cause his death. It must have felt like being slammed by a tsunami of depressive thoughts triggered by his comedown—also known as "the crash."

Fortunately, I didn't take my life that morning. Instead, I came to a new understanding and with it, a newfound compassion. And I realized that neither compassion nor understanding alone would resolve my grief, that coming to grips with Nils's suicide would take time.

For a year after that moment in the carport, I continued to live in our home, desperate to stay close to Nils—his clothes, his music, his office, his workout space, even his briefcase, every remnant of the life we'd shared. Of course, intellectually I knew that he had died, but it was as though my brain and my heart weren't speaking to each other. For months, I walked around the house looking for him, at times needing to remind myself he was *really* gone. At night—still searching—I'd go out to the driveway, lie on the ground, and look up at the stars.

Nils, a shy, childlike, emotional, and brilliant man with a wide range of interests, was fascinated by science. We'd talk for hours about quantum physics, string theory, and parallel universes, and now as I lay there in silence, I wondered which star Nils was. At other times, I'd sit admiring the palm trees that lined both sides of the driveway and talk to him. *Palm trees in Switzerland?* Yes, we had palm trees at our home.

Nils had been as enigmatic in life as he was in death. He loved this world and most everything in it. He was an explorer at an early age. While still in high school, he wanted to see America and found an exchange program in Torrance, California. When I asked why he chose California, he said because it was far from Sweden and near the ocean. He lived with the school's football coach and his family, studied hard, practiced sports intensely, and enjoyed the beach as often as he could. He was touched that complete strangers opened up their home to him. He became fond of them quickly, learned about generosity, and fit in perfectly.

One day after school, a couple of girls invited him out for ice cream, he told me, but he declined. He was more interested in playing American football. He blushed, even after all these years when he told me this, confiding that he'd wanted to say yes to the girls but was just too shy.

During his semester abroad, he learned a lot about who he was and what he was capable of. His love of travel and experiencing other cultures had been ignited. Although we didn't know it at the time, when Nils was in Torrance, I was in Santa Monica, just twenty minutes away. We both believed it was destiny that we met decades later on the Caribbean island of Antigua. He told others that his life had come full circle when he married a California girl.

While an exchange student, he fell in love with palm trees, so much so that decades later when he purchased a home in Switzerland, he had them imported and planted along the sides of the driveway. To him, they represented strength and flexibility, and reminded him of his life-altering experiences as a young man in Southern California. He also loved that he was the only one of his neighbors who had palm trees.

He was also passionate and fascinated by everything associated with aviation. He loved that he could work anywhere in the world, needing only his MacBook, iPhone, and earbuds. He enjoyed that his work as a venture capitalist required him to travel to different countries, stay in luxury hotels, and spend time in airports. So, he had bright blue lights installed along the driveway to give it the feel of a private runway. After Nils died, I turned the runway lights on every night, convinced he was among the stars looking down and would see them. I wanted to guide him home. I wanted him with me. And even more, I wanted him to see the light, the beauty in this world he had shown me. Nils taught me that magic is possible—that you can have palm trees in Switzerland and dream big.

But now, all I felt was grief and confusion. On May 8, 2011, the day Nils walked into the carport to end his life, life as I knew it changed radically. Grief comes without warning, and as the American Hindu guru Ram Dass, who wrote the book *Be Here Now*, said so eloquently, "It burns its purifying way to completion." Grief didn't send a warning flare. It didn't place a courtesy call before showing up at my doorstep. It broke through the door indifferent to the suffering it would bring in its path of destruction and ravaged its way through our home, leaving pain and devastation in its wake. The worst of all houseguests, grief moved in, stayed way past its welcome, and almost burned down the house.

Grief can take the form of paralysis or stagnation, a sense of being trapped with no way out. Wrapped in my own darkness and out among Nils's stars, I began to take small steps toward the light, no longer consumed by this black hole of grief that had torn through me when Nils ended his life. Over the next few years, as I passed through many stages of grief, pain, and fear I'd never imagined possible, I tested the limits of my psyche. I had faith, lost it, and reconnected with it again. I heard voices as though they were real, and then my mind became quiet again.

Finally, I surrendered—or was I forced to surrender? Like so many survivors of a loved one's suicide, I was in the depths of despondency and hopelessness, and discovered that Grace, too, is always there—in the brightest and darkest of moments. Grace is an unearned gift and spontaneous. By Grace, I was able to move through it all and stay sober. I did it one day at a time, and in the end, I not only survived but feel as though I'm *sparkling like a sapphire in the sun.*

✳   ✳   ✳

As though prescient, my aunt Lucy sent me a powerful email two days after Nils's suicide that helped guide me through my grieving. Three decades earlier her son, my cousin Tyler, had died in a car accident—he wasn't wearing his seat belt—and she withdrew from life. Despite our not having been in contact for over fifteen years, she was kind enough to reach out because she had been where I was heading.

> *Dear Kim,*
>
> *I am deeply sorry for your loss and only wish to send you condolences and something from my heart.*
>
> *You are in the midst of one of the most painful and trying experiences that a human can possibly endure. No one can know the depths of your pain, and I know that you will never forget this terrible tragedy. Memories of your departed loved one will never leave you, nor should they.*
>
> *Hope for the future. . .*
>
> *I think it may help you to know that grief is a process, a long journey of acceptance and healing. And you can get through it and come back in time to have a happy and productive life. I know it is hard for you to believe right now, but you must hold on to hope, and keep in the back of your mind that things will eventually get better.*
>
> *You are not alone in this. You probably feel overwhelmed and bewildered right now, like you were picked up and placed on a*

*different planet. This grief thing is a surreal new world of
uncharted territory, and no one gives you a road map.*

*This tidal wave of grief overtakes you, smashes down upon
you with unimaginable force, and sweeps you up into darkness
where you tumble and crash against unidentifiable surfaces only to
be thrown out onto an unknown beach, bruised and reshaped.
Grief is overpowering and universal but it is survivable.*

Peace be with you and God in your heart.

All My Love

Aunt Lucy

*   *   *

I wrote this book to honor my late husband, Nils Nilsson. My intention
in sharing our story is to help others who have lost a loved one to suicide or addiction. No matter where you are in the journey of grief, treat
yourself with gentleness and get into action and you'll not just get
through, you will discover how sharing your story will benefit others.

I also wrote *It's All Grace* for those who have survived a suicide
attempt, are considering suicide, or are struggling with addiction. I
know you may be suffering, and I offer my experience as an acknowledgment of your pain, and a way out, which inevitably is *through* it.
Please ask for help and consider the harm you'll inflict upon those you
care about most, including yourself. There are no shortcuts through
depression, addiction, or grief. We need to show up every day and call
on radical self-love, self-compassion, forgiveness of self and others,
and patience. Ultimately, we can experience and embrace the gift of
Grace, which is always present.

I love my late husband despite the manner in which he died. And I
survived, I healed, and I continue to heal. I've been able to rediscover
peace and joy in the process. More than anything, I want to help others
who are feeling as alone and adrift as I felt, to find peace and joy, too.

And finally, I want to share a glimpse into my life, our life as a
couple, and the life of Nils, a beautiful, soulful man who once loved life

and left behind devastation, which I experienced as the aftermath of a tornado ripping through a village. Nils's life is memorialized in this book not by his action that day but by who he was his whole lifetime.

As we know, suicide is an unchangeable response to a temporary problem. Addiction and mental health issues can be treated. No matter what is happening today—good or bad—it will pass; and with the encouragement and support of friends, family, professionals, advisers, support groups, and even this book and me, you can survive. You can flourish. You can be free from the incomprehensible suffering you may be feeling and move from powerlessness, grief, fear, blame, anger, and resentment to love, abundance, gratitude, and redemption—*sparkling like a sapphire in the sun*—and realize that Grace is with you and has been, through it all. I will share how I did it as a road map of sorts, and I hope you, too, will find your way to the light.

CHAPTER 1

Unknown Grace

In a real dark night of the soul it is always three o'clock in the morning.

— F. SCOTT FITZGERALD

A fter the 12-step meeting that Sunday morning, Pierre, a family friend, encouraged me to join him and a few other friends at a sweet outdoor café, so I did. They felt strongly that Nils might get sober again because of what had happened the night before. As I was finishing my coffee, a chaotic energy surged through my body, and I felt as though I were being summoned home. So, I excused myself and off I went. Nils and I hadn't spoken that morning, which was unusual. When I left the coffeehouse, there was no missed call or text from him, so I thought he was probably still sleeping. I called Debbie, my sponsor, and she encouraged me to stay grounded when I spoke with him. A *sponsor* in the 12-step program is a mentor, someone you trust implicitly, typically the same gender as you, who has been in recovery for a good length of time. They help guide you through challenging times and celebrate the good times as well. Her parting words to me before I arrived home that early afternoon were, "I will pray for him."

Twelve-step programs are mutual aid organizations for the purpose of recovery from substance addictions, behavioral addictions, and compulsions. The fellowship is a community that follows a set of guiding principles outlining a course of suggested actions to help you

1

recover. It is a spiritual process, and you're encouraged to believe in a higher power. It can be God, the sky, the stars, the fellowship, anything you can turn toward when you need help, clarification, or simply to say thanks. It's often called a "power greater than oneself."

When I arrived home from the meeting, I parked outside the driveway gate, which was unusual; normally I opened the gate and parked inside. As I walked up the walkway, I saw Nils in the carport near his exercise equipment and felt a sense of relief that he was working out. But when I took another step, I saw that he was hanging from the rafter! To this day, I remember exactly what he was wearing: the short-sleeved pink T-shirt I'd bought for him in New York a few months earlier, his favorite Gap blue jeans, the black travel socks he was famous for, and his white Adidas tennis shoes, which he was quite proud of. My mom had given us matching pairs of Adidas shoes a few years earlier, and we often wore them at the same time.

My purse dropped out of my hand and I ran to him, while phoning Pierre to call an ambulance. I wrapped my arms tightly around Nils's thighs and lifted him as high as I could to ease the tension on his neck. I just screamed—for help, for God, for pure expression—for what felt like a lifetime. Our housekeeper came running from the guesthouse, and she began screaming too. I asked her to move my car so the ambulance could get through. It was all so overwhelming that only later did I realize I could have asked her to help me get him down. I continued to hold on to Nils, easing the pressure on his neck, and imploring someone to come and help. A tall muscular man and a woman came running up the walkway, and they were able to get Nils down. Immediately, the man began to administer CPR.

My heart felt as if it had been ripped from my chest. I cried tearless cries in utter silence, and could barely stand or breathe. When Pierre came running up the driveway, the man told him to step aside. The woman asked her husband to stop the CPR because it was clear that Nils wasn't breathing, and he told her, "You don't stop CPR until the ambulance arrives," and he kept on.

The police and the ambulance arrived at the same time. Paramedics ripped off Nils's shirt and began doing CPR themselves. At that point, I walked out to the front yard and screamed. I couldn't speak. I couldn't cry. I was shaking convulsively, having a tough time standing, and I just fell to the ground. A female police officer came over to console me, but I didn't want to be touched. She was desperately trying to calm me down, saying he was going to be all right. Pierre picked me up and insisted we sit on the porch together as we watched the paramedics continue to work on Nils. We sat as though suspended in time.

The paramedics were able to get Nils's heart started, and they rushed him to the nearest hospital, Hôpitaux Universitaires de Genève. I still couldn't think, speak, or feel anything rational. I just kept repeating to the officer and Pierre, "I was going to tell him how much I loved him when I got home. I was going to tell him how much I loved him when I got home!" I spent the rest of the day at the intensive care unit, where the doctors were trying to save Nils's life.

Dr. Yvan Gasche, Nils's primary physician at the Intensive Care Unit (ICU), encouraged me to go home for the night. I begged him to let me stay, to crawl into bed with Nils, to read to him all night long and play his favorite music and remind him that we had so much more to do together. He looked at me gently and said, "Please go home with your friends and get a good night's sleep. The ICU is extremely busy with loud machines and staff coming and going throughout the night. You will not get any rest here." *A good night's sleep?* I wanted him to make it all go away. I wanted him to fix Nils. I begged him for a miracle. He said he couldn't perform miracles but that he was doing his best. I collapsed into his arms and just cried. There was nothing more to be said.

I wanted to take refuge in "a power greater than myself." At the time, I was a practicing Catholic, *so I referred to this power as God.* I had thought my faith was unshakeable, but almost immediately I had a morass of conflicted feelings about God and my many spiritual teachers. It surprised me that I didn't lean into God but instead held Him accountable and preferred not hearing a word about God, or faith.

I reluctantly went home that night, and the next morning, I walked into our living room, grabbed every book about spirituality I had on the shelves, and threw them in the garbage can outside. Then I walked up the stairs, grabbed audiobooks by Wayne Dyer, Tony Robbins, Esther Hicks, and Eckhart Tolle, and threw them away, too. *I've wasted decades studying about love, service, compassion, living in the present, focusing on what you want, and being a good person. And they're all full of shit!* Since I couldn't have a sit-down conversation with God about why good people die a brutal death or why He was too busy to intervene that day or whether He simply discarded Nils like trash, I took my powerlessness out on books about God and spirituality. I was enraged at God. Nils's action was God's ultimate betrayal. If He was all-powerful and loving, He failed Nils's kids, his family, and everyone who loved him, including me!

Shortly after tossing the books away, I rushed to see Nils, who was still on life support; and Jack, a friend from the Geneva 12-step fellowship, joined me at the hospital so I'd have someone to lean on. I was also receiving text messages from others offering to help. I spent as much time as I could sitting with Nils, running my hand through his hair, reading about a world event, and holding his hand. When I took a break, Jack and I would sit together on the floor in a quiet corridor of the hospital. The ICU waiting room was filled with other loved ones waiting patiently for some news about their family member. The day felt like an eternity.

On the third day in ICU, Dr. Gasche called me in to a small private room and told me Nils was brain dead and would need to be taken off life support, that there was nothing more they could do. He held my hand and just looked at me with his gentle blue eyes. I told him he was mistaken and demanded that he collect Nils's things and discharge him. I was adamant and said I'd be taking him home. He looked at me and said, "That will not be possible, Kimberly." I felt paralyzed. There was a deafening silence in spite of my mumbling and trembling. He grabbed hold of me and held me tight.

Nils's kids and family arrived shortly after I received the news, and we all spent time with him, saying goodbye. I begged Dr. Gasche to let me stay with him until he took his last breath. He stressed that he was brain dead and wouldn't know I was there, that it would be unpleasant once the breathing machine was removed, and that it'd be best if I go home and wait for the hospital to call. I felt a responsibility to stay. I wanted Nils to feel loved and safe. Dr. Gasche and Jack, on the other hand, wanted my last memory of Nils to be of him looking very much alive with color in his cheeks, and I reluctantly agreed.

Before leaving the ICU, the head nurse asked me to collect Nils's things—sneakers, T-shirt, jeans, watch, belt, wallet, and wedding ring—but I couldn't bear the thought of receiving all that was left of the man who had been my husband. I thought that if I didn't collect his things, someone in the hospital would come to their senses and tell me it was all a big mistake. Jack grabbed my hand and we walked together down several long corridors while passing doctors, nurses, visitors, and patients. There was a lot of commotion, and there was also utter silence as though everything was happening in slow motion. As we stood at the window, Jack explained to the administrator why we were there. She asked for my identification before handing me the brown paper bag. Then he kindly but firmly guided me to the hospital chapel to pray for Nils.

I watched him get down on his knees, fold his hands, and devoutly bend his head in prayer with the brown paper bag between us. He looked so sincere and emotional. *Where the hell is God, Jack?* I thought. *How are you able to keep your faith at a time like this? If I were to pray, who would I pray to? Not Jack's God; He's the One that bailed on Nils.* Though we were both Catholics, he seemed to have a connection to the Divine. I thought that because of his ability to pray, coupled with his faith, it might all become undone. Perhaps the doctors would come and tell us they had made a mistake.

Jack and I left the hospital and reconnected with Nils's family at our house, and we waited for the call. The kids were playing table tennis and the others were sitting at the kitchen table talking. Jack and I sat outside quietly. The call came around 10 p.m. on May 10. Nils had stopped breathing. Jack prayed aloud for Nils's soul and thanked God for taking care of him. I sat next to Jack suspended in time and speechless. It took half an hour before I could muster the energy to walk into the kitchen to tell them. You could hear a pin drop.

Obviously, Jack's prayers hadn't worked, at least not in the way I had hoped. No amount of prayer was going to bring Nils back. Prayer simply doesn't work that way.

In the coming days and weeks, I appreciated when people told me they were praying for me, but I asked them to pray for Nils. I disliked when they suggested I pray to God. *The God that watches people suffer? The God that would let a husband and father commit suicide? Where was God when Nils climbed up on the paint bucket and wrapped the dog's leash around his neck? Where was God when Nils was calling for help? Where was God when I found him? Where was God when a stranger was giving CPR and then the EMTs and doctors were working on him?*

I needed answers and began reflecting on my past . . .

*   *   *

Being raised in a religious home, prayer was a regular practice for us on Sundays. My mother was Catholic, my dad Lutheran. When I moved to Santa Monica at age five, we lived near St. Paul's Lutheran and St. Monica's Catholic churches, which were a block apart. We attended St. Paul's most often, but I loved the lavishness of the Mass at St. Monica. Attending services on Sundays was mandatory for us kids until we turned eighteen. The emphasis was on tradition and ceremony rather than spirituality.

In college, I started exploring other spiritual practices. I learned about Judaism, Orthodox Christianity, Islam, and Buddhism. When addictions to cocaine and prescription pills took hold in my early twenties, my interests in spiritual matters took a back seat to getting high and being obsessed with what I was eating or not eating. Still, I always kept a beautifully framed picture of Jesus in my house and a bronze statue of the Hindu god of dance called Shiva that I found abandoned in my alley. I knew very little about Hinduism back then but it played an important role later in my life. The spiritual properties of both the photo and the statue may have contributed to my surviving my addictions. When I was using, I was oblivious to the possible dangers I was exposing myself and others to. I was so busy getting loaded that when the Los Angeles riots started in April 1992, I was unaware of any of it. I called my brother and asked him to help me score some coke on the streets, because I had run out and my dealer was on vacation. I purchased drugs only through reputable sources.

My brother was sober at the time (for which I had no regard). He and I jumped into my beautiful new Mercedes and headed directly to Venice. The streets were like a ghost town, and a little man on a bicycle rode by and told us to get the hell out of there. We didn't listen and proceeded toward a group of people standing in the street. As we arrived, someone started shooting at our car and someone else threw a Molotov cocktail through the window, and it hit my brother in the head and splattered blood everywhere. The windshield was shattered. I stepped on the gas, but I didn't drive my brother to the hospital. Instead, I drove back to the hotel where I'd been staying, put a damp cloth on his forehead, laid him on the bed, and continued looking for cocaine. It was a miracle we survived. I had put my life and the life of someone I loved at risk for a fix.

My parents tried many times in many ways to help me get sober, to no avail. They thought I might end up a statistic—dead from using and from my eating disorder. One intervention included getting involved with an organization called Youth with a Mission for six months. YWAM is an international movement of people of all cultures, age groups, and Christian traditions dedicated to serving Jesus. Their common purpose is to know God and make Him known through missionary work throughout the world. My dad helped me complete the application so I could be approved for the Discipleship Training Program, which seeks to bring you closer to God. Phase one of the training is the lecture phase, and phase two is the outreach phase. I was approved for a six-month commitment, three months in Honduras and three months in Jamaica. The night I left, I'd been up for several days doing cocaine and pills. My parents knocked on my door, packed some clothes, drove me to Los Angeles International Airport, handed me a one-way ticket, and said, "Go get well."

As I walked off the plane the next morning in Norfolk, Virginia, I saw my name on a sign held by two very energetic people, Debbie and Bill. I wasn't sure whether to run away or acknowledge that I was Kimberly. Despite my trepidation, I walked up to them and introduced myself. I was too exhausted not to. They drove me and several others to a large ship, the *Anastasis*, which we all boarded. There were people of many ethnic backgrounds and skill sets, from doctors, dentists, disaster-relief specialists, and lots of enthusiastic young people. I was feeling seriously uncomfortable, coming off a cocaine high and unsure about being there or what was going to happen next.

The following day I was escorted to a room of about thirty men and women sitting in a large circle introducing themselves. They all shared a love of God and the desire to become ministers or missionary workers. Sitting there coming down off a several-day run, I wondered what I would say when it was my turn. I wanted to come up with a really great story, because the thought of telling them that I was a drug addict did not seem to fit the situation. I was extremely nervous and grateful I would be among the last to share. I couldn't run away; the ship had already left port and we were sailing toward Honduras.

A miracle occurred that morning. By the time they got to me, I told them the truth. I burst into tears and told them that I was suffering from a cocaine and pill addiction and frankly wasn't quite sure why I was here. They all jumped up, laid hands on me, and prayed for me. It was a bit overwhelming, but I felt safe. Bill and Debbie had to confer with a few others to decide whether I should stay or go. They agreed there was a reason I was there, and I was allowed to stay. The organization and the individual members' passion for God and being of service turned out to be life transforming for me.

The experience reconnected me with God in a space that was both intense and playful. The worship music was contemporary, soulful, and joyous. Being exposed to poverty and being of service to the locals in Las Mangas, Honduras, and the Black Hills of Jamaica helped me under-stand the difference between a need and a want. It taught me about being of service to those truly in need, sharing one's faith and hope, and loving unconditionally. The villagers and the volunteers I met during these six months had a profound impact on my life and on my using.

I would like to say this was the event that got me sober, but it wasn't. My family came to the port of San Pedro, outside Los Angeles, and picked me up. It was an emotional reunion. Mom and Dad looked peaceful and were happy I was home and sober. Within a few days of being back, they whisked me off to a meeting to celebrate my six months of sobriety. I stood at the podium and received my six-month sobriety coin and thanked God and my family for my sobriety.

Within forty-eight hours I was back living with my cocaine dealer. My using escalated and my eating disorder became extreme during the next couple of years. My immersion with YWAM was still in my heart and haunted me. My using was never the same, because I'd had a taste of freedom and what it was like to have a personal relationship with God.

Fortunately, my dad did not give up on me and did one final inter-vention, and I agreed to get help. I literally crawled into treatment at age twenty-eight. You hear about people who are highly functional for long periods despite their using. Oftentimes, these people do finally hit a wall and get sober. I was not a high-functioning addict, which helped me get sober at a young age. I was in a recovery home for four months and lived with eleven other women, most of whom had spent time in prison for drugs, prostitution, and crimes they'd committed while under the influence. I was scared straight.

I was formally introduced to the 12-step fellowship during this time, which helped me become reacquainted with my faith. After com-pleting treatment, attending weekly meetings became a priority and I began going to early-morning Mass again. I loved the pageantry and grandeur of the Catholic church. It was calming and grounding. I also had a friend named Vegas who was a Soka Gakkai Buddhist, and he encouraged me to chant the mantra *Nam-myoho-renge-kyo*, assuring me that it wouldn't interfere with my Catholicism. At first, I was concerned I would be struck dead for participating in another path, but instead, my ideas of faith and spirituality began to expand. I was no longer in fear of God; for God became my friend. God was, for the first time, accessible, humorous, and easy to communicate with, much like the missionaries and students in my YWAM adventure. For me, this was transformational. The two faith practices seemed to coexist perfectly and even balanced each other.

At the time of Nils's death, my higher power was still God, and I also believed in karma as I understood it. Nils wasn't what I'd call a traditional believer, but he seemed to enjoy my talk of God. We had long conversations about the role of faith and prayer in our lives. Nils hadn't grown up in organized religion, so he didn't raise his children in any particular church. But he was a seeker, always open to growing. A few years before we met, he was introduced to Kabbalah, an ancient wisdom that reveals how life works, and he devoted a fair amount of time learning about it.

The word *Kabbalah* means "to receive." It is the study of how to receive fulfillment, addressing ontological questions—the nature and purpose of existence—and presents methods that help in attaining spiritual realization. Nils found Kabbalah to be an intelligent practice and enjoyed wearing a red string on his wrist to remember that there is a power greater than himself. Several months after we met, he offered to put some red strings around my wrist, which I eagerly agreed to. It reminded me that I'm not in charge, but God is. I still wear a red string on my wrist.

Nils's main "spiritual" practice, though, was science. He believed in parallel universes and multiverses. He studied quantum and string theories. He believed one could be dead in one universe while living a full life in another. Reading about the significance of the atom in Bill Bryson's *A Short History of Nearly Everything* brought Nils to tears. He found his "God" in the wonders of the universe and its perfection, and was overcome by our miraculous planet and the grand, creative design of the universe. He looked as radiant when he talked about science as others do when they talk about faith. Since he thought praying to God was silly, I asked him, *What do you do when you struggle? Who do you pray to?*

"I just say the problem out loud," he told me. "I let the universe know what's going on." For him, the universe was there to support us, even though he believed we lived in a universe that was unfriendly at times. I, on the other hand, lived in a convivial universe and was always surrounded by kind, extraordinary people and phenomenal opportunities. I was conscious of the many miracles in my life. Nils believed that we as individuals have to take responsibility for our own lives. And when he died, I wondered, *Where were you, Science? Where were you, Universe?*

Nothing prepares you for the spiritual abyss you are likely to enter when a loved one commits suicide. Nothing prepares you for the feeling of someone you love being ripped from your life. Before Nils's death, prayers provided a sense of comfort and of knowing all issues would be resolved. After Nils's death, I had to embark on a new journey, experiencing a new level of despair. *How can I pray to God if I don't believe He's there? How can I find my way out of this darkness? If Nils doesn't "believe," what's become of him?*

I became obsessed with where his soul was. I wondered if he might be trapped in some multiverse, and if so, *How would I find him in the afterlife?* And speaking of the afterlife—*Can someone who commits suicide go to heaven? Is there even a heaven?* I was terrified that, because he had killed himself, his soul would be damned for eternity in a dark, cold, mean-spirited place filled with the souls of Hitler and the like.

Another belief that challenged me arose from my study of Buddhism. *Karma* is the spiritual principle of cause and effect, where intent, thoughts, words, and deeds influence outcomes. Every cause brings an effect. I had practiced Soka Gakkai Buddhism (chanting Nam-myoho-renge-kyo) for ten years, and I wondered, *What karma had Nils set in motion with his manner of death?*

I sought assurance from Buddhist adepts and was told that death is the last state of existence in this body. When the eternal energy leaves the body, it returns to the universe as potential energy waiting for the right circumstance to reappear in this or another universe. Buddhists are grateful to be born as a human because it is in human form that one can plant positive seeds for the future. In so doing, past causes that may manifest themselves in this lifetime can be resolved. I felt comforted that Nils's spirit was probably not suspended somewhere unpleasant. He had been a kind and generous man in this lifetime, and I believe he had planted a lot of positive seeds despite the way he died.

Vegas encouraged me to start chanting again, even a few minutes a day. Through chanting *Nam-myoho-renge-kyo*, he said, I could have a positive impact on Nils's karma. So, I chanted a little each day. It's a vigorous practice. You hold prayer beads between your palms while reciting the words. I continued to struggle with demonic visions and needed more assurance that Nils's spirit had gracefully, or not so gracefully, moved on to wherever it was supposed to go.

Finally, I decided to meet with a Catholic priest, Father Richard at the Notre Dame Church in Geneva. I explained the situation and asked him point-blank if he thought Nils's soul was in hell or somewhere in limbo. He assured me that God is loving and forgiving, and that God knew his heart at the time of his fatal action. He also suggested that some actions humans take aren't voluntary. I burst into tears and sat quietly for several minutes, knowing that Nils's spirit was not shackled in some scary, dark place and he was not being tormented for not having a personal relationship with God or Jesus.

Father Richard could see that I had a heavy heart and was feeling guilty for not being able to prevent Nils's death. He asked me if I wanted absolution. I shared and confessed all the irrational thoughts I'd been having since Nils had died and asked God to forgive me. It seemed appropriate since I was with a Catholic priest and desperate. I also shared with him a moment that had been haunting me. While on a ski trip in the French Alps just a few months before he died, Nils skied up beside me and then told me he occasionally thought of hurting himself. Wanting to make sure I heard him, I took off my ski helmet and asked him to repeat himself, which he did. I asked what he meant, and he said that sometimes he wanted to ski so hard that he would harm himself. I asked if he had thoughts of killing himself, and he said, "*Nej*," Swedish for no. He said it was more like pushing his abilities to the limit, that he loved the rush when he took calculated risks. Nils had done a fair amount of heli-skiing, which can be very dangerous. It's off-trail downhill skiing from places reached by helicopter rather than by chair lift. I thanked him for being vulnerable with me, gave him a bear hug, and encouraged him to consider seeing a therapist to explore further what he had confided in me. He declined and said that sharing his thoughts with me was good enough.

If I could turn back time, I would have insisted he see someone. Father Richard prayed for me and made it clear I had done nothing wrong and now I had to forgive myself. "Kimberly," he said, "forgiving yourself will take time as will reconciling how you feel about God. Just give it time." Even though I knew it was perfectly normal to feel disillusioned by God's unwillingness to intervene on that fateful day and to feel guilty even if there was nothing I could have done, I was grateful for his perspective. Being encouraged to feel whatever I needed to feel was hugely important and healing.

A few days after meeting with Father Richard, I was fumbling around the internet, still wondering about the whereabouts of Nils's soul, and I came across a book titled *Life after Death*, by Deepak Chopra. I had attended a talk by Deepak about what happens to the body and soul when we die. He'd said that a part of us never dies, a core consciousness (soul) that is eternal—timeless—and nonlocal. The physical body dies because it's "local" in space and time. Deepak said that he believes life as we know it is a projection created in our minds and that we have to die to the past in order to create a new future. His eyes lit up as he told us that he himself was looking forward to death. Remembering his sentiments brought me some comfort and a brief respite from worrying about Nils's soul, because I was able to see death as a transformation into something new, and from this perspective, I could begin to believe Nils's soul was free.

But moments like those were fleeting. In the ebb and flow of grief and confusion, one minute I'd feel comforted knowing where Nils's soul was and then suddenly, waves of panic and doubt would overwhelm me. During one of these times, I went to see a London clairvoyant who was staying outside Geneva. I knew it was a bit odd, but I felt pulled to do so, and I simply had to know where Nils was and that he was okay. I brought Nils's wedding band with me. As she opened the door, it felt as though I were walking into a time portal. Her reddish-blond hair was pinned up but still wild and unkempt. She could have been a caricature of a fortune teller, or a hippie who'd just stepped out of 1969.

She invited me into the living room and asked me to sit across from her at a table with a jeweled cloth draped over it. Without speaking, she pulled out cards and began reading them aloud. It was uncanny how spot-on each card was, how much it related to my life, and I was immediately drawn in. She told me someone very close to me had recently died, and I said I'd just lost my husband and was concerned about his soul in the afterlife. She asked if I'd brought anything of his, and I handed her Nils's wedding band.

She closed her eyes for a moment, then opened them suddenly. She'd had a vision. She was able to recount Nils's last day—including his final moments—without me sharing any of the details. It was similar to the vision I had had of Nils's final moments. She said he had desperately tried to correct his actions but was unable to stop it. I was stunned.

Then she moved me toward a massage table, where she did a kind of energy clearing. At one point, she moved away from me and sat on the edge of a console table, where she began swinging her legs back and forth like a child on a large chair. I was taken aback. When Nils would sit on something similar, he'd swing his legs exactly like that. Then she told me: *Nils is here. He's in the room right now,* and she spent a few minutes talking to him. For a moment, I felt his presence, maybe because this clairvoyant was so adamant that he was there, but I don't think so. *I felt him.* He whispered ever so softly in my ear that he was sorry for leaving and causing me so much pain and suffering. He explained that he had tried to stop it but couldn't. He asked for my forgiveness and reminded me how much he loved me and that he would always be with me.

This was no hallucination. We hear what we are ready to hear, see what we are ready to see, and feel what we are ready to feel. I must have been ready, as I so wanted a connection with him. No tears were flowing from my eyes, but my heart was filled with the gentle rain of my soul. I softly expressed my eternal love for him and that I forgave him. I knew my friends would think I was crazy, but it was what I needed to do to feel some peace and comfort so I could get to the next moment, the next day, and the day after that.

*   *   *

I had so many profound experiences of healing and peace during the first year after Nils's death—but they were like butterflies in a windstorm. They were just *moments*, but they added up and helped me take tiny steps toward healing, despite the lingering frustration, doubt, and confusion. I call these surprising moments of peace, clarity, and volition—even in the darkest of times—*Unknown Grace*. Although I was unaware of it at the time, Grace was with me throughout these dark times, guiding, comforting, holding, and steadying me.

One morning in particular just three or four days after Nils had died, I found myself overcome with grief and collapsed on the kitchen floor against a cabinet. As if pulled or pushed, I can't say which, I reached over to the doggie drawer and opened it. I put my hand in the drawer and pulled out a piece of paper with "The Promises" from the *Big Book*,[1] the main text describing the 12-step fellowship with forty-two stories of men and women who have recovered from addiction. I had no idea why this copy of "The Promises" was in a kitchen drawer, let alone the doggie drawer; I had no recollection of putting it there. I began reading it aloud:

If we are painstaking about this phase of our development, we will be amazed before we are even halfway through.

---

[1] Bill Wilson, et al. *The Big Book of Alcoholics Anonymous.* 4th edition. (New York: Alcoholics Anonymous World Services, 2001), 83–84. First published in 1939.

Promise 1: We are going to know a new freedom.

Promise 2: We will not regret the past nor wish to shut the door on it.

Promise 3: We will comprehend the word serenity.

Promise 4: We will know peace.

Promise 5: No matter how far down the scale we have gone, we will see how our experience can benefit others.

Promise 6: That feeling of uselessness and self-pity will disappear.

Promise 7: We will lose interest in selfish things and gain interest in our fellows.

Promise 8: Self-seeking will slip away.

Promise 9: Our whole attitude and outlook upon life will change.

Promise 10: Fear of people and of economic insecurity will leave us.

Promise 11: We will intuitively know how to handle situations which used to baffle us.

Promise 12: We will suddenly realize that God is doing for us what we could not do for ourselves.

Are these promises extravagant? I think not. They are being fulfilled among us—sometimes quickly, sometimes slowly. They will always materialize if we work for them. Even in the darkest of days, I knew I was being held and guided, and that I was going to stay sober throughout the grief process. These are the moments I call Grace.

The promises reminded me that despite the unspeakable pain and grief, this experience would ultimately benefit someone, that at some point, something good would come of this nightmare. I felt as if I were being hugged or placed in the palm of someone's hand, wrapped in a sense of security, knowing I would survive. I realized in that moment I would not allow myself to become a bitter widow. I also knew I had to let myself experience the dark emotions. I was assured it wouldn't happen overnight—I would have years ahead of me—but somehow, some way, I knew I was going to be okay.

Grace is like that. It's given freely and unmerited. Grace arises for sinners and saints, with the lonely, the suffering, and the bereft, as well as the joyful, the happy, and the hopeful, for junkies in the bowels of the city and yogis secluded in an ashram, for those who committed suicide, those who considered suicide, and those sitting on the kitchen floor deciding to live.

I have come a long way since those early days and weeks and months. At times, all I could manage was to sit on the floor in silence. Some days I quietly raged; on other days I prayed. There is no linear path or timeline out of grief. What I knew, even though I had a host of doubts during this period, was that I was being held by an Unknown Grace. My body and mind were weak, but my spirit was wide open to receive all the Grace that was pouring into me. Now, my higher power feels like *Energy*. It's unifying. It's in everyone and everything. In essence, we are God. God is no longer outside me. It's a beautiful energy that can be experienced in all living and nonliving things. And this Energy was with Nils too. Even in his darkest moments, even in his despair, he was being held.

In late 2012, after nineteen months of recovering, I met an amazing man named Craig, who patiently and lovingly gave me the space and support I needed to continue to move through my grief. With Craig, I began to explore a new dimension of spirituality through Hinduism. He invited me to Laguna Beach, California, to meet his friend Swami Vishwananda, who is considered a spiritual teacher. He thought that having a private meeting with him might help me, so I went. My meeting with Swamiji was simple and to the point—love is beyond words. He also promised to assist Nils in the afterlife. In addition, there was a small private *satsang* (spiritual gathering) that involved some singing and receiving a *darshan* (blessing) from him. Leanne, a close friend of Craig's, was kind enough to guide me through the experience. The feeling of unity and love, and a sense that all was well, permeated the evening. Today, she is one of my dearest friends, too. We are transparent with one another and laugh every time we speak. I love the wonderful surprises that come from blindly saying yes.

A month or so later, Craig was leaving for India with some friends and encouraged me to join them. He also planned to reconnect with Swamiji. My heart was already there, but I was not always trusting my decisions. I told him I'd have to contact Cynthia, my sponsor, and ask what she thought. Without hesitation, she said, "It's India!" I shared our itinerary, which would include Varanasi, Rishikesh, and the Maha Kumbha Mela, and she responded, "*Go, go go!*" She told me India is the most spiritual place on the planet.

Craig and Cynthia did not know each other at the time, but both were active practitioners of *bhakti* (devotional) yoga, and, it turned out, they knew many of the same people. *Bhakti* also means participation, fondness, homage, faith, love, devotion, worship, and purity, and it goes hand in hand with the 12-step philosophy. *Yoga* means union. It's a practice that strives to join the individual self with universal consciousness, the Divine. Many who engage in a spiritual life direct their prayers to a particular God, whether Protestant, Catholic, Muslim, Jewish, or other monotheistic or Abrahamic faith. Hinduism is considered a polytheistic faith that expresses God through many faces, including Ram, Krishna, Ganesh, Hanuman, and Lakshmi. The followers are seeking different things like guidance, protection, and blessings—through them. They each have different gifts, like Lakshmi, the goddess of knowledge, morality, beauty, courage, prosperity, and long life, and Ganesh, the elephant god who symbolizes protection and the remover of obstacles. Hanuman represents devotion and strength. The deities were appealing to me because they are artistically beautiful, with an abundance of color, and because they represent love, hope, and strength. Hinduism was also appealing because it offers so many options to choose from, for it is not linear. The deities I ultimately connected with felt like old friends.

I reached out to my parents, as they knew how excited I was about broadening my spirituality. My dad was confused by my need to go, but my mom encouraged me to do whatever I needed to put my life back together. Wanting her to feel comfortable about me traveling so far from home with someone I hardly knew, I arranged for her to speak with Craig first. They had a great conversation, and before I knew it,

Craig and I were on a plane to India with his friends Huner and Adrianne. It was early 2013.

Our trip began in Varanasi, on the banks of the Ganges River, one of the most sacred sites in India. Hindus go there to die. To be cremated on the riverbank is considered a great blessing. Thousands arrive every morning at sunrise to bathe in the waters of Ganga, believing they will be blessed with good luck; others come to pray. Some tourists believe that just visiting Varanasi brings them blessings. The area is quite death-positive and full of rituals for accepting and even celebrating death.

The streets of Varanasi were teeming with people walking or riding bikes, motorcycles, and rickshaws, considerably busier than midtown Manhattan. There was so much energy in the air, and a beautiful spiritual stillness as well. We connected with Swamiji at a small local shop, and he invited us to join about fifteen of his devotees on a boat ride on the Ganges to offer flowers in remembrance of loved ones. A devotee is someone who shows interest in and respect for someone or something. I've been a devotee of self-improvement and inner development most of my life. We felt blessed to be invited to join this ceremony and spend time with Swamiji and his devotees in this holy setting.

Late in the afternoon, we boarded a large wooden boat and pushed off into the holy river. Standing next to me was a lovely devotee, elegantly draped in a white sari, named Anuprabha, and she asked, "Who will you be thinking of when you set that beautiful dish of flowers on the Ganga?" I briefly shared what had happened with Nils and that I was taking a leap of faith that this small action might help him find his way home. We made an immediate connection, and we're still close.

As the bright-red Indian sun was setting, the boat stopped in front of a *ghat*, a sacred staircase alongside the river, where the dead were being cremated in an open fire. I could hear the beautiful bells ringing in the distance, as bodies were brought to the site and burned in sacred ceremony. Loved ones, neighbors, strangers and workers, each holding a handful of flowers and a candle, were praying and celebrating the soul's life and death. It was a gorgeous ritual; I was in awe of its simplicity and purity.

Time stood still. Then the captain of our boat gave each one of us a dish of colorful flowers with a lit votive candle and encouraged us to celebrate our loved ones who had died, by placing our flowers on the river as a symbol of our love and with faith that their spirits had moved on. I looked across the boat and saw Craig standing upright, all in white with his right hand on his heart. He was smiling from ear to ear as he gently nodded to me. I could feel a divine energy in that moment—it was electric, it was Grace. Several people on the boat were singing a Hindu *mantra* (a song repeated as a meditation) that elevated the sanctity of the experience and welcomed the presence of those who had passed away. They sang *Om Namah Shivaya* over and over in a slow, practically hypnotic way. This mantra is imbued with sacred power and can lead one directly to their heart and bring about a sense of inner and outer peace when recited. I was able to feel all this while witnessing the rituals at the burning ghat, and it was deeply consoling.

Then I placed a dish of flowers on the water and thanked Nils for loving me and for all he had taught me—how to laugh, be in the moment, and treasure every experience. He loved me with passion and fervor. He was funny and kind, magnanimous and adventurous. He was and always will be my love. He was and always will be pure light and joy. The candle I lit in his honor was so bright that it lit up the water. This was no coincidence; for Nils's light always shone bright while he was alive, and it was clear that it was still shining like a sparkling sapphire in the sun. I smiled as I looked up at the full moon and felt Nils's presence all around me. After searching for Nils's soul, I was surrounded by pure love, energy, and Grace. And in that moment, two years after Nils's passing, I realized the answer to my question: *Yes, there is life after death.* Life for me. Life for Nils. Life for his children. The darkness I thought Nils was trapped in disappeared, and all that was left was light and energy—pure, beautiful, and bright. And I *knew* this experience of light was possible because of the darkness I had experienced for so many months. How best to see the light, but in the dark?

CHAPTER 2

Facing Fear

Fear is present when we forget that we are a part of God's divine design.
Learning to experience authentic love means abandoning ego's insistence
that you have much to fear and that you are in an unfriendly world.
You can make the decision to be free from fear and doubt and
return to the brilliant light of love that is always with you.
Who you really are is that unclouded love.
— DR. WAYNE DYER

My journey back to love and light was extremely challenging. Along with grief and depression, I grappled with *fear*. From the moment Nils was pronounced dead, I became terrified of nearly everything. Life as I knew it was unrecoverable.

I called my mom as soon as I arrived at the hospital. It was Mother's Day. She asked me to repeat what I'd said several times. She too was in shock. I had called believing she could fix everything. Of course, that was irrational. But when I heard her say she couldn't undo what had been done, I went into a panic. *Living life without Nils would be impossible. Our lives had become entwined. We had developed a healthy dependence on each other; he was my best friend, my soulmate, my guide, and my protector.*

Shortly after speaking with my mom, I received a call from someone who was clearly distraught, telling me that Nils had phoned earlier that morning saying he was going to drown himself in the lake. The caller felt guilty and shaken about their last words to him, which were

"Go ahead and do it." Their feelings of guilt resonated deep in my bones, because I, too, was feeling somehow responsible for leaving him alone that morning.

The other difficult calls I had to make were to Nils's parents and sisters in Sweden. I spent several hours on the phone with them, at the same time trying to make sense of what was going on. Just the night before, Nils and I were having dinner with the kids and enjoying each other's company, and now I was standing in the lobby outside the ICU talking to his family about him possibly dying because he'd attempted to kill himself. I urged them to come to Geneva immediately, which they did.

I was terrified of living without my best friend and of the unknown. I began having anxiety attacks, symptoms throughout my body that felt like heart attacks. I went from feeling safe and secure—the wife of a loving husband—to being utterly vulnerable and alone, and I didn't know what to do or who to turn to.

To make matters worse, unbeknownst to me at the time, Nils had some less-than-trustworthy business associates. Nils's hospitalization made headlines in Sweden, and in the days following his death, theories began to circulate that the Russians he'd been doing business with had him killed. I received calls from Swedish reporters to confirm that Nils was found hanging and asking if I thought the Russian mob was responsible. I desperately wanted to believe that rumor, but I knew it wasn't true because of the drug that was in his system and the phone calls he'd made that morning. It would not have changed the shock and anguish of him being gone, but it would have lessened the mental torture of him taking his own life. Learning that some of his business associates were unsavory only amplified my angst.

I knew nothing of Swiss law and a family friend suggested I identify "a protector" immediately, someone to look after my interests and speak with counsel and the notary overseeing the estate process, because I had no idea what was coming and I was, to say the least, fragile. This was great advice; however, my real protector, the person I trusted the most, was no longer alive. I felt like I was on a fast-moving train that had lost its brakes. I was an American legally domiciled in

Switzerland with no experience navigating any estate process, let alone how it's done in Switzerland.

Swiss law is complex. Though Nils had a will, I seemed to have few rights. The government froze our accounts. *How will I support myself? Who am I if I'm no longer Nils's wife? What am I going to do?* My mind raced with all sorts of morbid forecasts.

Still in shock, I had to deal with finances, attorneys, and a completely foreign process, and with all the communication in French. Nils's assets were reported to be in the millions, and his Russian "friend and associate" claimed Nils owed *him* millions of dollars. Another "friend and associate" made the same claim, that Nils owed *her* millions of dollars. I was dumbstruck. Nils had never told me any of this. These claims seemed to be coming out of the blue. Fortunately, Nils had cautioned me about both these people, and sure enough, as soon as he died, they descended on the estate like vultures. The woman had a will that Nils had made two decades earlier, and she hired a Swiss attorney to contest Nils's current will. Ultimately, her petition was disallowed. In addition, I attempted to determine the value of some of Nils's assets and was threatened more than once by one of his business associates that if I didn't stop trying to help the estate, there would be consequences. I began to fear for my life, and I notified the Collonge-Bellerive police.

Along with fear, I felt an overwhelming sense of betrayal by people Nils had thought of as trustworthy friends. For them, Nils as a human being was an afterthought. This was new territory for me, and I had no idea how to deal with them. Fortunately, most of his business associates *were friends* and acted honorably, but a few did all they could to get a share of his assets now that Nils was no longer here to declare what was true. I was becoming withdrawn and afraid of others—and myself.

✴   ✴   ✴

Most people who are in grief, especially from a sudden death, can't just go off to a retreat center or even a corner and cry all day. There are the usual day-to-day responsibilities and the one-of-a-kind tasks following a death.

At times I hid under a blanket in our bedroom's walk-in closet, where I felt safest, even for brief periods. But there was much to do—so much uncharted territory to cover. I was unprepared for the chaos and for the ease with which you can be taken advantage of when you're that vulnerable. Overwhelmed by the demands and discouraged about it all, I didn't know who to trust or what to do. Even some of the people the estate hired to assist seemed to be taking advantage of the situation.

I was forced to engage a notary, a legal expert, to oversee the estate process, and from the get-go, he seemed interested only in receiving a sizable retainer before his summer vacation. At my first meeting with him, he allowed the attorney who represented the person with the out-dated will to attend, which was clearly a violation of privacy. This attorney looked me straight in the eye and said, piercingly, "You were the last person to live with the deceased. Is there any money?" I said, "The deceased has a name—Nils Nilsson," and I got up and left the room. I was drowning in all that was going on around me. In hindsight, I should have identified a protector, as my friend had suggested.

My sleep was erratic. Many nights I just wept, and I was afraid to share my anxiety with my family because they were far away and struggling with Nils's sudden death themselves. It forced me to rely heavily on my friends who were in the 12-step program—as well as the postman (yes, the postman). I became increasingly afraid to open mail or emails. The mailman knew this, because some of his deliveries required my signature. So, he'd drive up on his yellow scooter and wait patiently at the gate till I reluctantly buzzed him in, and then he'd have tea with me and translate the mail and even emails from French to English. He was kind—a saint, really—and incredibly generous with his time, making sure I understood everything before he'd leave. With a smile on his tanned face, he was always happy to see the dogs and me. I was grateful for his help during those challenging months.

I found the idea of having to start over terrifying, yet I managed, with help, to muddle through the complicated layers without causing damage to myself or others. Because a number of volatile people were threatening to get their way, I felt compelled to take action even in this tender state. It felt like walking through a minefield blindfolded, and I was grateful for friends who surrounded me with love.

The spiritual teachers and philosophies I follow encourage us to take action when we're afraid—which is different from acting out—and in doing so, to acknowledge, embrace, and learn what is beneath the anxiety while still moving forward. I remembered when I'd gotten certified as a skydiver. On many trips, terror would well up through my body and stay there as I drove to the drop zone, got in my gear, entered the aircraft, jumped out of the plane alone, free flying, pulled the parachute cord, and then faced the dreaded landing. I say *dreaded landing* because I only landed on my feet a dozen or so times. It was challenging to master when to flare the parachute to slow down the landing. The feeling of terror coupled with jolts of excitement was my pervasive experience during skydiving. I remembered that I'd grown exponentially during this time because I leaned into my emotions instead of letting myself be devoured by them.

With this in mind, I knew I had the tools to face whatever was in front of me. I'm a "toward" person rather than an "away" person, and still there were moments I just curled up in the closet. In the aftermath of a suicide, doing the untenable can interrupt the healing process. Self-care is paramount, the ground from which all action can grow.

Helen Schucman's *A Course in Miracles,* whose theme is that love's presence is the greatest miracle, states, "All healing is essentially the release from fear."[2] The *Course* is a self-study program designed to awaken us to our oneness with God and Love, offering a psychological-spiritual path that brings joy, peace, love, an understanding of self and others. This has been my experience, and I can see why those moments when I was gripped by terror, mistrust, and a lack of faith in others or myself delayed my healing. Fear challenged my trust in a higher power and the idea everything would

---

[2] Helen Schucman and Bill Thetford, *A Course in Miracles* (New York: Viking/The Foundation for Inner Peace, 1976), chap. 2, sec. IV, 7.

work out for my highest good. Ultimately, everything did. Throughout it all, I was discovering valuable lessons that allowed my soul to grow and heal, and I would journey from suffering to survival to sparkling like a sapphire in the sun.

But at the time, all I knew was that the pain and fear felt very real. The *Course* also states:

> *Tolerance for pain may be high, but it is not without limit. Eventually everyone begins to recognize, however dimly, that there must be a better way. As this recognition becomes more firmly established, it becomes a turning point. This ultimately reawakens spiritual vision, simultaneously weakening the investment in physical sight. The alternating investment in the two levels of perception is usually experienced as conflict, which can become very acute. But the outcome is as certain as God.*[3]

Yes, the outcome *was* certain—these fears would eventually be released because most were an illusion. But before they could be, everything had to fall apart—or as the *Course* states, "become very acute"—for me to realize that everything was actually falling together.

---

[3] Schucman and Thetford, *A Course in Miracles*, chap. 2, sec. III, 5–10.

CHAPTER 3

Everything Is Falling Together

*Everything can be taken from a man but one thing: the last of the
human freedoms—to choose one's attitude in any given set
of circumstances, to choose one's own way.*
— VICTOR FRANKL

Nils's suicide and its aftermath were my personal Twin Towers. Just
as I thought things couldn't get any worse, another "plane" came
crashing from out of nowhere and everything around me felt as though
it was collapsing into oblivion. When Nils died, I naively thought everyone in his life he loved would join *together*. I thought I'd be bound for life
with his family because of our shared love of Nils. I thought his parents
would always be a part of my life, because I loved them and had a close
relationship with them. They had always thought I was a good influence
on him—coparenting, communicating, and helping him stay sober. Even
though I was on shaky ground after his death, I believed I would be okay
because of the love we all had for Nils. I was wrong.

Throughout the time Nils and I were together, he had joint custody
of his kids. We traveled the world together, played together, learned languages together, celebrated holidays and birthdays together, and were
very much a family. One of Nils and my favorite holidays was Christmas—decorating the tree, wrapping presents, stuffing stockings, hanging colorful lights, and singing carols. Nils introduced me to Anne Sofie
von Otter, who sang "Home for Christmas," a gorgeous carol in Swedish

and English. It was one of Nils's favorite songs and became one of mine. We played it all day long on Christmas, and I still love listening to it.

My mom, known as Nana to the kids, needlepointed beautiful and whimsical Christmas stockings for each of them. On what would be our last Christmas Eve together, my mom and Nils filled the kids' stockings with goodies and leaned them against the presents that surrounded the base of the Christmas tree. I secretly filled his stocking. The following morning, he was surprised and delighted to see that my mom had made him a stocking with a telemark skier on it. A kid at heart, he loved Nana.

Nils owned a Santa Claus suit, and it was a heartful experience watching him put it on, grinning from ear to ear with the red furry hat with white fluff and his white beard. It was a wonderful tradition that had begun when his kids were very young, and he was determined to keep it up even after the kids knew who he was because of his black military boots. Eventually, Nils's Santa suit was given to them, knowing it would bring a lot of joy when they would entertain their own children.

We prepared simple meals together. The kids loved pasta, chicken fingers, and *pommes frites*. Nils on the other hand wanted more stimulating meals. One of my first Christmas gifts from him was an iPod with several seasons of Jamie Oliver's cooking shows. I had no idea who he was, but they all did. At first, I thought it was a joke, but it was no joke. I learned to cook, among other dishes, Indian food, which he loved. I helped the kids learn English, and that was a lot of fun. I became a parent-teacher association (PTA) volunteer at Emma's school, which gave me a chance to see her once a week at school when I was in charge of reconnecting students with their lost items. We watched movies on the couch in the den together. We must have watched *Transformers* two dozen times, and Charlie never tired of it, nor did I. Mia turned me on to the hit TV show *Dexter,* which we watched all the time, and I got to tuck the little ones in at night. We spent a fair amount of time in the VW family wagon—to and from school, and also to the stables while Emma and Mia listened to Lady Gaga and Katy Perry. We had our conflicts and differences of opinion, like who would help with which chores, and what qualified as a clean room, but there was kindness, love, and silliness as we were figuring it all out. I was grateful to be accepted by the kids.

Then, not long after Nils's memorial, his ex-wife called to tell me not to see the kids anymore. *What!?* My body tightened, and my heart felt ponderously heavy. I asked her to repeat what she'd just said, and she did. I was so unable to let the words in, I asked whether the little ones would be coming over that afternoon. She raised her voice and repeated that I was no longer permitted to see her children. After a long, eerie silence, I asked her why and she said she had to get off the phone. It was devastating! Not only was I facing the loss of Nils and our home, now I was losing the children too. Things seemed to be getting worse.

But there was more. I wanted to continue to have a relationship with Nils's parents, to see and talk with them regularly. They had become a part of my family, and most important, they were my late husband's parents. But when I called, they rarely picked up. When I wrote, the letters were returned to me unopened. Finally, a year after Nils's death, his father called, blaming me for his son's death. It's challenging for people to understand and fully comprehend how shocking and out-of-the-blue a suicide can be unless you've been through it, so I shared with his dad the last couple of days of his son's life, hoping it might help.

On May 6, 2011, two days before his suicide, Nils woke up in a great mood and excited about the day, which was typical for him. The garden was bursting with colorful flowers, the sky was azure, and Lake Geneva was sparkling. He asked me to spend the day near him, and he included me in several important business calls. We went for a late-morning run and lay on the grass just snuggling, rolling around like kids, and saying how much we loved each other. I said, "I love you more today than yesterday," and he grinned widely, saying he was grateful I was in his life and that he couldn't imagine life without me.

He looked playful yet serious as he often did when he was working. In the afternoon, he said, "I'd like to tell you everything that's going on."

I kissed both his cheeks, his forehead, and his lips while looking deeply into his eyes and said, "I trust you and believe in you." I went directly to the kitchen, grabbed my purse, and went off to pick up the little ones at school. I still periodically wonder if, had I listened to what he wanted to share, his heart would somehow have been unburdened. I'll never know. All I know is that I did trust and believe in him.

The day before Nils died, he was happy, as usual. He took the little ones to the gym, had lunch with them, and bought them sneakers. He called me four times to express his joy at being a papa, his love for his children and for me, and how grateful he was for the life he had. Nils, the kids, and I enjoyed an early dinner together. The children talked about their day in detail. Mia was excited about some music she had downloaded and played the tunes for us. She was interested in a new boy at school, and Clara was teasing Charlie as usual. With a mixture of English, Swedish, and French, there was a lot of laughter and a sense that everyone had had a great day.

After dinner, Nils and the children went outside to play. I noticed that Nils seemed a little off. He was looking at the sky as though amazed by something, but then his attention would return to the soccer game. I asked if he had taken anything, and he said, "*Nej.*" He said he was feeling tired but was, overall, in great spirits. I asked again if he had taken any-thing, and he said, "*Nej,* Kimberly." Doing my best to adhere to the sug-gestions in a book I read called *Getting Them Sober,* a guide for those who live with an alcoholic, I walked away. It was difficult, but I did it. I knew that challenging him wouldn't help. He wasn't intoxicated, he just seemed slightly off. I went inside, tidied up the kitchen, and called someone in the program to see how she was doing.

Nils's oldest daughter, Emma, arrived home around 9 p.m. and asked if she could go to a party. She was really excited about it, and Nils offered to drive her. I suggested she call her mom to drive her because her papa seemed slightly off and may have taken something earlier and shouldn't be driving. They spoke in Swedish for a few moments, and Nils made it clear he was fine to drive and sober. Nils told me again that he hadn't taken anything, and there were no physical indications that he was impaired. His communication was clear and articulate. It was just an intuitive sense. As they drove away, I had a bad feeling in my stomach.

An hour later Emma called, hysterical. She said her papa was unable to drive and she'd taken the keys from him. I encouraged her to call her mom and ask her to pick them up, as I had the other three children at home. When they arrived home, Nils was barely able to walk. I'd never seen him in this state. Nils's ex-wife was upset with me for letting Nils drive while intoxicated and allowing Emma to be with him. I assured her he appeared to be sober, just slightly off in temperament.

Pierre, who had been living with us, helped me get Nils on the couch in the den. We checked his vitals and watched him for a bit. We discussed taking him to the hospital but decided that he just needed to sleep it off. Before Nils's ex-wife left, I let her know I'd be leaving for my support-group meeting the next morning, Sunday, at around 9:30. I had a commitment at this particular one. Pierre would be going to the meeting as well and thought it best that I go and get spiritually centered before talking with Nils. The kids were picked up early Sunday morning. I felt conflicted about leaving Nils to go to my meeting, but I also thought it was important that I take care of myself.

Even though I did my best to explain to Nils's father that he was not intoxicated when he got into the car to drive Emma to the party, he refused to believe me. I stressed that I had done everything I could to keep him safe and was totally confused by what had transpired. He said that I shouldn't have gone to the meeting, blaming me for not stopping Nils's suicide. Knowing the outcome, I felt tremendous remorse for going and not being there when Nils needed me the most. I had great empathy for Nils's dad, and I understood that he'd lost his only son.

I also shared with him that just a few weeks earlier, on April 22 (my birthday), on our way home from Dubai on what would be our last flight together, Nils gave me a birthday card during the flight that had his thirty-day sobriety chip in it. It was the best birthday gift he could have given me. He seemed humble and grateful, and appeared to be back on the path.

I knew that when I got home after the meeting that fateful Sunday, we would have to talk about the night before—the simple fact that he could have killed himself and his daughter, or an innocent bystander. We would enact a plan for him to get sober that may have included going into treatment. I would tell him how much I loved him and that I was willing to go to any lengths to help him. I was hoping this would be the turning point and that he would go to whatever lengths were necessary to get sober. I believed the near-tragedy the night before from his using would propel him to get sober again.

But Nils's dad wanted nothing of it. He was also angry because I hadn't asked him what to do with Nils's body. His parents had wanted him back in Sweden. I told him Nils wanted to be cremated, his ashes spread on Mont Blanc, and that I honored their son's wishes. It was clear he needed someone to blame and nothing I might say could help.

A few months later, I made one more attempt. I called Nils's mother and expressed a desire to see them before I moved back to the US. She politely declined: "It's not a good idea for you to come." I felt discarded, but understood their grief. Nils and I had spent many wonderful weekends with them in the southern part of Stockholm. Not only would I miss our communication—I talked with his parents at least once a week—I'd miss being in their apartment, surrounded by photos of their children and grandchildren. I'd miss hearing Nils and his father sharing stories at the kitchen table.

One story was about Nils not obtaining his university degree. He had just one final economics paper, and he didn't turn it in. He felt it wasn't good enough. Knowing Nils, I'm sure the paper was excellent. Nils loved to tell this story in front of his dad because of the hubbub it created. His dad would add that he knew Nils's professor. Nils enjoyed any attention he received from his dad, who still encouraged him to complete his degree after all these years. It was sweet to hear them tease each other.

Nils also got a lot of pleasure teasing me in front of his parents. He enjoyed leaving on all the lights in the house, and I would walk by a room with no one in it and turn off the lights. Nils called me the Princess of Darkness, which made us both laugh. His parents were good sports and would laugh even when Nils repeated the same stories. I missed these long chats, taking his parents' dog for walks, going out to lunch with them, sharing a piece of *prinsesstårta*, Swedish princess cake, and shopping with Nils's mom. Losing contact with them was, to me, another death.

The life I'd known and cherished was collapsing all around me. During these times I'd call my sponsor, Debbie, often in a state of panic. She was all in. She'd take my calls and patiently listen to me describe my world falling apart. Then, calmly, she would say, "*My love, it's all falling together.*" How could losing Nils, his children, and his family be a good thing? So, I said it again, "Debbie, I'm losing everything! *Everything!*" and she'd tell me again: *Everything is falling together.* So, as the world around me was falling apart, that became my mantra: *Everything is falling together, Kimberly. Everything is falling together.*

Debbie wasn't delusional or heartless. She knew *exactly* how much Nils, his children, and his family meant to me. She was simply a calm, wise presence with twenty-five years of sobriety behind her, and she was able to help me see what I knew instinctively to be true—that Nils's ex-wife and Nils's father's responses had little to do with me and more to do with their own pain and self-protection. We were each grieving in our own ways, and I was responsible only for my own.

With Debbie's guidance, I was able to see his ex-wife's response in a new light. It must not have been easy to watch her children bond with another woman. She might also have felt that cutting me off was in the best interests of her children. She saw how distraught I was. I now believe she wanted to protect the children as much as possible from all the turmoil. Debbie encouraged me to forgive her, to hold the children in my heart, and to let go—for their sake and for mine.

I had to do the same with Nils's father and mother. The more I tried to hang on or reach out, the more pain I was causing them and myself. I needed to trust that not spending time with them was in support of everyone's highest good, and though I couldn't see it yet, something positive would come of this. The key, Debbie said, was that I stay sober, be of service, and do the next right thing, and I would see everything more clearly with each passing day. This, coupled with living respectfully and maintaining faith in the fellowship, which never let me down, kept my head above water. In fact, it became my higher power for a while. Some people and the traditional ideas I had about God had failed me initially, but trusting the divine, unfolding *process* never does. By doing the work, going to meetings, sharing honestly, and taking one day at a time, I knew that everything would—eventually—work itself out.

When Debbie said, "Everything is falling together," it wasn't a vacuous statement. She didn't say there would be a pot of gold when all was said and done. She reminded me that we're powerless over other people, and that I couldn't arrange everything to my liking. That's not how it works. I had to stop trying to manage outcomes and let go of results. Some people drive themselves crazy—or to drink—by attempting to control people, places, and things. It's impossible, as Debbie reminded me. I couldn't control what others thought of me or their perspective on what had happened. I needed to let go of the impulse to explain myself and the desire to put everything back in place. That wasn't going to happen, and I was only creating more suffering by trying to resurrect a past that no longer was.

Debbie reminded me regularly that life without Nils and all that it entailed was the new normal. She also reminded me that my life was still full and had plenty of people to lean on. I had the fellowship, my friends, and my family, who all rallied around and supported me, and I had my higher power who, over time, would take a new shape in my consciousness. She encouraged me to focus on what was coming together—friends, family, and newfound interests—and that through these things I would see small changes and some movement forward, step by step.

She never suggested I'd be free of panic and grief, that I'd miraculously wake up and be free from pain and suffering. But her advice to take one day at a time and gain some patience, perspective, and new understanding did help. I could send love and light to Nils's family whether we spoke or not. I could love them from afar and to want the best for them. I deeply understood their grief, for their lives had been turned upside down. She encouraged me to pay attention to signs in my own life affirming all was falling together. The Promises suggest that we take responsibility, act with integrity, and trust that whatever we're going through will eventually benefit others.

So, I threw myself into exploring grief and death, to address my *own unanswered questions*. I enrolled in a grief counselor certification program through the American Academy of Grief Counseling, where we read dozens of books and wrote papers on death and dying and the grief process, which helped me get more comfortable talking about them. Though I was getting emotional support from family and friends, I needed an intellectual understanding of my own and others' grief. Reading provided insights into my own pain and the pain of others. It helped me realize that what I was experiencing was fairly common, that sudden deaths, and especially suicides, can create an explosive situation. In addition, other losses in one's life—like divorce, a career change, the death of a pet, or the sale of a home—that haven't been fully processed can be reignited, which provides the opportunity to heal those as well. Feelings that were dormant like jealousy, insecurity, and indifference often arise. The tendency to draw a line in the sand or to blame others is completely natural. Having a cognitive understanding along with emotional support helped me reach new levels of growth and, at the same time, see that I had plenty of work left to do. If I wanted things to "fall together," I had to deal with my own dark emotions, including the urge to blame others for Nils's death.

CHAPTER 4

Who to Blame?

*All blame is a waste of time. No matter how much fault you find with another,
and regardless of how much you blame him, it will not change you. The only
thing blame does is to keep the focus off you when you are looking for external
reasons to explain your unhappiness or frustration. You may succeed in
making another feel guilty about something by blaming him, but
you won't succeed in changing whatever it is about
you that is making you unhappy.*

— DR. WAYNE DYER

After a suicide, the urge to blame others can be overwhelming. The
idea that someone we love chose death over us is unimaginable,
especially if it wasn't preceded by a long period of depression and suicidal ideation to cushion the blow. I remember the day in December
2010 when Nils read in the *Wall Street Journal* about Mark Madoff,
Bernie Madoff's son, hanging himself with a dog leash in his New York
apartment. He had sent an email to his wife saying that she and their
child would be better off without him. Nils and I talked about Mark's
action and the suffering he left behind for his wife, children, parents,
siblings, and friends. Nils said that Mark's toxicology report would be
available in a few weeks, but it didn't appear that drugs or alcohol were
involved. He said that Mark must have been deeply ashamed of his father's behavior. I asked Nils if he ever thought of suicide, and he admitted that he'd had dark thoughts like that while under the influence but

it had been a long time ago. I sensed that Mark Madoff's story had resonated close to the bone for Nils, but then it faded from my mind.

Nils's suicide, by all appearances, was impulsive. He didn't leave a note. He never spoke about being suicidal and hadn't given any indication that he was. From what I now know, it is clear that it was drug-induced. In the days before his death, Nils was busy being Nils—smiling, joking, filled with energy. He was excited about a couple of conversations he'd had with Swedish childhood friends about a new business venture, and seemed genuinely happy spending time with his beautiful kids. How could someone who seemed to have it all—a loving wife, wonderful children, a challenging career, parents and siblings who adored him, good friends, and a life most would be envious of—want to take his own life?

Nils underestimated the power of his addiction. Sobriety was not the most important thing in his life, and after he relapsed, he might as well have been playing Russian roulette. So, when Nils's father blamed *me* for his death, I felt his pain and had compassion for him. He needed someone to blame; the painful truth that it wasn't anybody's "fault" was simply intolerable.

I, too, had a compelling impulse to blame—to blame God (or my *idea* of God as judge and jury, Father and Decider). God decided who lived and who died, who would be saved and who would be damned, who would suffer and who would get to be happy. This Father God's unbridled power, as I understood it, had been a source of confusion for me for many years, watching good people suffer and horrible people cause harm and get away with it. I believed there is a heaven and a hell, but did bad people really go to hell?

Nils was a good man and was surrounded by people who looked up to him and adored him. Why should his loved ones have to suffer this horrific loss? Why should Nils suffer? I felt so deeply betrayed. God had abandoned Nils and all those who loved him. *Blaming God* was a welcome distraction that made me feel a little bit lighter.

In the end, though, I had to acknowledge that it was Nils, not God, who had ingested cocaine and taken his own life. Nils had been "the decider." I had to accept that the man I loved had let me down. He'd promised over and over that we would live the rest of our lives together, that we'd take our last breaths together, like Noah and Allie in the film *The Notebook*. And instead, he left me alone. I felt that God had abandoned Nils, and Nils had abandoned me.

So, the need to blame him felt almost involuntary, but since he had already paid the ultimate price, I blamed myself, others, and even inanimate objects. There were some extreme moments when I felt I deserved to die because I hadn't been able to save him. As a passenger on the motorway, I had thoughts of unbuckling my seat belt and jumping out of the car. Thoughts like these were fleeting, but extremely intense. Daryl and Jack took me to a local fair in the center of Geneva a few months after Nils's passing with the hopes of boosting my spirits. Before I knew it, Jack took me on a ride called Around the World. It was like a carousel with seats for two, and it twirled around as it climbed higher and higher until we were overlooking the tallest buildings in Geneva. He was terrified, clutching the safety bar with white knuckles. I, on the other hand, was sitting calmly enjoying the view while noticing that I could easily lift the safety bar and jump to my death. It was comforting to know I could end the pain so easily. If Nils had thoughts like that, he probably didn't take them seriously or, I believe, he would have shared them with me. Sometimes, without warning, I felt the urge to destroy something that Nils had valued. I thought about burning down the house to make Nils suffer. I was consumed by the need to hold someone or something responsible.

From our bedroom window, I could see our beautiful garden, and also the supply room where we stored gasoline. One particular day, I walked down the stairs, through the kitchen and across the driveway into the supply room, and grabbed a can of gasoline when suddenly I heard a voice say, "The house has stone walls; it will not burn." So, I stopped myself.

My next thought was to burn the garden. *That will show him,* I thought. Nils loved the garden, so it seemed perfectly sensible to destroy it. And the same quiet yet firm voice said, "You have to sell the house." As I put the gas can down, I spotted a large pair of shears, and I grabbed them and began pruning every tree and ripping out the weeds with my bare hands. Thankfully I didn't burn down the house or destroy the garden. But it was a close call. I not only might have gone to jail but could also have put my life and the lives of others in danger.

After that, weeding and pruning became a great outlet when I felt powerless. As I yanked out the weeds, I expressed my uncensored feelings toward God, Nils, and the others. In other moments while gardening, I spoke softly to Nils, as though he were standing next to me. I expressed sorrow, unhappiness with his choice, and compassion. I told him that someday I would come to terms with what happened, but right now I couldn't. The pain was too raw.

Like many who lose a loved one to suicide, especially abruptly, I wasn't merely confused, I was *furious*. I wasn't just sad, I was *despondent*. I wasn't simply afraid, I was *terrified*. I didn't just feel tired, I felt *exhausted*. Nor did I just feel hopeless, I felt *unhinged*. Every feeling was magnified a thousandfold. Grace—all of this is Grace, pushing us to our full ability to experience life.

When I told a friend about these near-tragedies, she encouraged me to call Father Timothy, a local Catholic priest, to perform a cleansing of the property. She felt it would help the house, Nils, and me. So, I called Father Timothy and asked if he'd do such a ceremony. He asked why, and I burst into tears, telling him what had happened and that a friend thought there might be demonic spirits on the property. The energy throughout the house felt heavy and dark. He agreed to come to the house and encouraged me to have a few friends there as well.

Father Timothy and another priest arrived the following day, dressed in black with the traditional white tab collar, Bibles in hand and a vessel filled with holy water. They blessed each room while sprinkling holy water, praying for the children by name in their respective rooms and for Nils and me in the master bedroom.

Then we gathered outside the front door, where Timothy, a rather large man, began pounding on the door and in a raised voice demanding the evil spirits be gone, while the other priest prayed and sprinkled holy water on the front door. This scared us all and at the same time seemed to make perfect sense. Next, we walked to the guesthouse. Starting in Nils's office, then the living room and the guest bedrooms, he blessed each space while sprinkling holy water. Then we went to the carport, where he sprinkled the water while praying loudly for Nils's spirit. There, the two priests pounded on the wall near the rafter and *demanded* that the evil spirits be gone. The hair on my arms stood up, and the energy on the property, in the house and the carport, seemed to change dramatically. It could have been my imagination, but it felt very real.

Despite the profound presence of these two holy men and the seeming efficacy of this experience, I still felt conflicted about God, some of my spiritual teachers, and my part in it all, too. There were still moments I believed it was my fault—if I had been a better person, God would have intervened. I'd spent years practicing the "law of attraction" principles, which are pretty simple—you create your own reality by what you focus on. Positive attracts positive; negative attracts negative. I had focused on Nils as my Prince Charming, believed deep in my bones we would be happily and lovingly married the rest of our lives, and instead I was a widow in my mid-forties. I felt that Abraham, the spirit that Esther Hicks channels, had been a false teacher. I was too distraught to acknowledge what I knew to be true: God, Abraham, and Nils were not to blame for the thoughts *I* was having. I listened to Wayne Dyer say that blaming others is a way to turn the focus away from our own suffering, but I wasn't ready to hear his next sentence, that *forgiveness is the way through*. I still had a need to blame others and myself, and that was that.

God had not protected Nils from himself or helped him get sober when he really needed it, and I was to blame for not acting swiftly enough the moment I found him: *What if I had taken Nils down from the rafter immediately? What if I had administered CPR? What if I'd stayed home that morning and not gone to the meeting? What if I hadn't let him drive his daughter that night?* My mind raced endlessly, consumed by guilt. I researched the mechanics of asphyxiation over and over, and still didn't know whether I could have saved his life. So, a few months after Nils's death, I met with his attending physician in the ICU, Dr. Gasche, to ask him whether, from a purely medical perspective, there was anything I could have done and specifically whether taking him down from the rafter as soon as I found him and doing CPR immediately could have changed the outcome. I needed to hear the doctor say that Nils had already been gone too long—that there was absolutely nothing anyone could have done to save him short of being there the moment he hanged himself.

When Dr. Gasche absolved me for not being able to save him, I beat myself up for leaving him alone that morning. *But who hasn't left their spouse alone? Who hasn't gone out?* I had no way of knowing he was suicidal. He'd never mentioned it in all our years together and there were no obvious signs, like being depressed for long periods, talking about death, showing changes in his personal appearance, withdrawing from daily life activities, or feeling hopeless. He was, however, reorganizing his finances due to a complex business decision, and he was a periodic substance user. I thought the worst that could happen was we'd have a difference of opinion whether he needed to go into treatment. And yet after he died, I beat myself up again and again until eventually, I realized the futility in blaming his addiction, his associates, Nils, God, or myself. Finally, I accepted that God didn't kill Nils, nor did I—*that Nils killed Nils,* and that cocaine played a significant part.

Despite having a regular spiritual practice that included Catholicism and approaches like Manifestation and the Power of Intention, I was catapulted by Nils's suicide into revaluating my whole life. As time passed, I could see how these spiritual philosophies were not at fault either, and that continuing to practice them would assist my healing, provided I could face my experience honestly.

I met with Dr. Gasche two more times, and then I started meeting with Father Richard to sort through my feelings. I knew I'd develop a relationship with God again at some point, and I hoped it might even transform into something more mature and majestic, that I'd be able to get back on my knees and pray. Somewhere deep inside I knew I was being cared for by something—I just didn't know what to call it. Father Richard reminded me: "God can take it. He can handle your truth." So, through Father Richard, I brought it all to God—all the pain, betrayal, and blame. Something inside me was shifting. I knew *within* that I had the resolve to transform my experience, even though at the time it seemed next to impossible. I was being given the opportunity to grow exponentially.

Now I look back at all the blaming with love and light. While blame is ultimately futile—it doesn't transform suffering, bring closure, or satisfy a sense of justice—I've come to see it is a necessary part of the process because it comforts the restless and confused soul that is searching for answers in the dark.

Following a loved one's suicide, we can feel wounded, victimized, and sad, and we want someone to suffer the way we're suffering. I journeyed from despondency to blame to righteous indignation, and even the desire for revenge, and it all distanced me from having to feel the inconsolable grief. Thinking the problem was outside myself, I could see it, touch it, wrestle with it, and through externalizing, find ways to move toward healing. There was Grace in blaming, an awareness and awakening in those times, too. A still, soft voice was guiding and holding me. When Father Richard said, "God can handle it," I felt embraced by the truth of *all* that was happening within me. Vegas continued to chant *Nam-myoho-renge-kyo* for Nils and me, to change our karma, and I held on to Vegas's belief that it helped lead us both out of a kind of purgatory. And absolution, which I needed so badly, came from an unlikely source: Nils's ICU doctor in Geneva. The blame and quiet rage that were coursing through me ultimately revealed: *This is how you grieve, Kimberly. This is how you heal.*

There is no perfect or saintly grief. As Ram Dass said so eloquently, "[Grief] must burn its purifying way to completion." And, there was still plenty of stuff to burn—red-hot anger and even vengeance.

CHAPTER 5

Anger and Revenge:
The Unspoken Feelings

Whenever we're challenged with anger, we have the opportunity to open to the difficulty and let the difficulty make us more compassionate, more wise. Or the opposite, which is that when things are difficult, the chances instead of it making us more afraid, and therefore more vulnerable or more subject to being able to catch the anxiety in the atmosphere and spin off into wanting to protect ourselves and our loved ones, and the tendency for aggression to escalate, and violence to escalate under challenge is much greater.

— PEMA CHÖDRÖN

Few people speak of suicide, and even fewer talk about the anger and feelings of revenge felt by those left behind. Beneath all the finger-pointing and blame, there is at its root a deep vulnerability, longing, and brokenness from which, during the darkest of days, there seems to be no relief. In fact, such emotions may lead to even stronger, darker ones like hatred, and these can be a lifeline from the torrents of grief. Many people who are grieving tell me they feel these intense and sometimes alarming sensations and emotions, and I tell them it's okay and that they can be a normal response to their situation, that their grief lives within and is doing its work as it moves through the darkness, just as it did for me.

I loved Nils deeply and was having a challenging time comprehending the enormity of the hardship that had descended on his loved ones. It was just too big. Anger, on the other hand, was accessible. These conflicting feelings began to reveal themselves at the funeral home only days after Nils passed. I could barely function, let alone make monumental decisions like what to do with Nils's remains or who to hire to help with the many tasks ahead. I had never been responsible for someone before in this way. The hospital provided a few referrals, and my friend Raushana helped me reach out to mortuaries and schedule the dreaded but necessary appointment to plan what to do with Nils's body. Raushana heard what had happened through a mutual friend and reached out immediately, offering to help in any way. She was a lifesaver. Pierre, Jack, and Raushana accompanied me to the mortuary. I tried to get out of going, but they all just smiled and put me in the car.

Nothing seemed real. Jack parked the car, and Raushana and Pierre walked me up a never-ending flight of stairs into the most depressing lobby. Pierre took my hand and literally *pulled* me up the stairs. I was like a child refusing to go to bed. I stopped several times; I physically couldn't move. But Pierre was patient and persistent. On our way to the funeral director's office, we passed rooms with names and numbers on a plaque, and it occurred to me there was a body behind each door, like a house of horrors. We were surrounded by death. This nightmare had become my life, and I wanted to escape, but Pierre and Raushana somewhat forcefully guided me to the director's office.

Monsieur Funeral Director sat down at his large desk and spent what felt like an eternity organizing his stapler, some papers, and some pens. I sat between Pierre and Raushana with my eyes fixated on the fancy urns on the shelf behind his desk. Some had photos of the deceased on them. Then I leaned over to Pierre and Raushana and said, "Nils doesn't deserve an urn. I want his ashes placed in a Ziploc bag." All three of them looked surprised, and Pierre gently held my hand and asked me to repeat myself, which I did. My exasperation was insulating me from the intolerable feelings of sadness and powerlessness. When Pierre realized I wasn't kidding, he told the funeral director in French what I wanted. The director looked shocked, adjusted his necktie, and said something in French as he wrote a note to himself.

I was drowning in feelings. Anger toward the director—and Nils—for subjecting me to this horrendous situation was percolating, and my thoughts began to race. *What do I know about funeral arrangements? Nils and I should be at home cooking dinner or working out, not selecting urns! I don't want my husband's face on a jar. I want my husband! I didn't ask for death to come into my life. I played by the rules, and it didn't matter.* I was feeling unhinged and began to shake.

Raushana and Pierre could see I wasn't well and spoke on my behalf in French, handling everything except signing the cremation authorization. When it came time to sign, I couldn't steady my hand. So, my mind reverted to magical thinking: *If I don't sign this form, we can go back to the hospital and pick up Nils.* I looked over at Raushana and Pierre and did my best to convince them there'd been a terrible mistake and that Nils was still alive. For a brief moment that felt like forever, it seemed like a real option. It took about twenty minutes for me to put my signature on the cremation request.

When reality struck—that Nils was actually gone—my seething subsided, and grief returned full-force. I wanted to become ash too, to be erased. I asked Raushana and Pierre to leave me there and that I would be okay. I wanted to be cremated with Nils. Raushana smiled kindly. I looked at the funeral director firmly and demanded he take me to Nils. The simmering agitation was back, this time directed at the funeral director. He stared at me as Raushana spoke to him in French, and explained that Nils's body was not at the funeral home yet and would be moved there in a few days. He explained that Nils no longer looked the way he once did and that it might be best if I do not see him that way. I began perseverating on the horrors of cremation and the realization that his physical body would no longer exist. Raushana and Pierre helped me up from my seat, down the stairs, and into the car. Jack suggested we have lunch together, and he drove to a small café. He and Raushana spoke of many things while I sat paralyzed, unable to express the layers of feelings swirling throughout my body and in my heart. I was exhausted.

A week and a half later, Jack and I returned to the mortuary to pick up Nils's ashes. On the way there, even though I was in the passenger seat, I found myself pushing my foot to the floorboard as if to step on the brake and slow things down. I felt that if we didn't go back and collect him, Nils might come home intact on his own. I kept these thoughts to myself, afraid that if I told Jack he might think I was going crazy. We walked up the same stairs, past the same rooms but with different names on the doors this time, took a seat in the director's office, and waited for Nils.

The director walked in the room with a sparkly blue bag, which seemed ridiculous, and inside the sparkly blue bag was a sparkly blue box, which he opened and then showed me Nils. He said Nils's name was written on a piece of tape adhered to the Ziploc bag. I simply wasn't prepared to see Nils this way. He put the top on the box, put the box back in the bag, and handed me my husband. I hugged Nils tightly as my heart burst into tears. I sat for a while just holding him close to my heart. When we got back to the car, Jack suggested we put Nils on the back seat, and I said, "Put him in the trunk! He doesn't deserve the back seat." I felt empowered, strong, and clear in the moment. As we put the sparkly blue box in the trunk, I realized they had chosen Nils's favorite shade of blue. Grace.

During those early days, weeks, and months, whenever my body and mind could no longer handle the grief and loss, I clung to feeling incensed—not just at Nils but at the whole situation and in particular toward the people I felt were responsible for his death. At that point in time, my anger was directed at two people Nils believed had taken advantage of him over the years. Because I was struggling with articulating my darker emotions, they festered, built up over time, and then manifested in aggressive and even violent ways. Here are a few stories: When my father came to Switzerland and told me that he had thought of killing himself and sometimes wished he had had the courage to do it, I slapped him. The release was almost involuntary. I did not have the capacity to hear my dad's truth in that moment. He was not trying to cause me pain—he was suffering as well. I just lost it, and I did apologize to him shortly after.

Several months after Nils's death, Pierre continued to be concerned about my well-being and thought it might help if I expressed some of my outrage. One morning as we were sitting on the deck having a coffee, he made an unkind comment about Nils to get a rise out of me. I asked him to say it again, and when he did, I started screaming at him and punched him in the chest. I was shocked by what I'd just done and looked him in the eye. Pierre repeated his words, and I punched him again. "Good, Darling," he commended.

He stayed the rest of the day to make sure I was safe and didn't do anything I'd regret. I broke garden pots in the supply room, threw rocks at the place Nils had hanged himself, hurled papers in his office, shredded his socks (except one pair of black socks) and underwear, cried, and shouted obscenities at the cocaine. Pierre sat there quietly, ensuring I would be safe while giving me the space to fully express myself. By the end of the afternoon, I was tired. The anger had indeed needed a release valve.

Appreciating what Pierre had just done, I was reminded of how Nils and I had met him. I was backing out of our snow-covered driveway one morning with all the kids in our VW family wagon and the electric gate swiped the side mirror off. The kids burst out laughing and said, "Papa's going to be mad." Together we all went to the VW dealership and were given an outrageously expensive estimate. A friend introduced us to Pierre, who replaced the mirror for a small cost, and he quickly became a part of our family and even moved in for a while.

I may have expressed and dissipated some of my frustration toward Nils and the cocaine, but I still needed to address my intense feelings toward some of Nils's business associates. What they had done and how I felt about them was my secret, and no one could take these feelings from me. Everything else could be snatched away in an instant, but the fury toward them was mine. In the fellowship there is a saying, "You are as sick as your secrets." We encourage our negative emotions to grow by focusing on them, which only fuels them. David Hawkins believes,

"What you hold in your mind tends to manifest. There is nothing magical about it. It's simply holding intention."

For a period of time after Nils's death, I elevated their culpability and convinced myself that these business associates *were personally responsible* for his suicide.

Eventually, these beliefs transformed into revenge fantasies that became increasingly real as the days went by. It took several months before I called my sponsor and told her what I was planning. I was able to describe in detail the flight I would take, where we would meet, how I would kill them and fly back to Geneva. I knew I'd be imprisoned and spend the rest of my life in jail.

In my mind, I'd have three prepared meals a day, would never have to worry about finances or fashion, and best of all, I'd be able to make a difference by establishing 12-step meetings in the European penal system. I could help people get sober and transform their lives. My life would have meaning. Not only would I avenge Nils's death, I'd be ridding the world of a few bad people and revolutionizing the penal system. *I'd really thought it through!*

I would be okay with whatever happened to me; all I wanted was for them to die painfully and know it was I who had killed them. I would shoot each of them six times—four bullets for Nils's four children, one for Nils, and one me. I wanted them to suffer in the way they were making Nils's children and me suffer.

During a moment of clarity, I confessed my thoughts to Debbie, and she advised me, wisely, "Kimberly, you'd better get on your knees now and pray your resentments toward them be removed before you do something that words or amends won't be able to correct." While I was living with my dark secret, it never occurred to me to pray, let alone forgive. Talking to her broke the spell and helped me see more clearly and truthfully.

Of course, she was right, but up until that moment, I wanted *someone* to pay for what Nils had done. I do believe it was a collision of causes that contributed to Nils's suicide: his relapse, the pressure he put on himself, the secrets he kept, and some of the business associates he was surrounded by. If he had made sobriety the most important thing in his life and hadn't used the global financial crisis and other business issues as excuses to get high, I believe he'd still be alive.

Confessing my desire for retribution was both therapeutic and cautionary. I realized how far my mind could take me if I let it go unchecked. Our thoughts are powerful. My negative thoughts drove my emotions, and they just grew and grew the way a watered seed blossoms into a flower. By talking to someone and expressing my plan, I could see I was in deep trouble. Just because I was having these thoughts didn't make them true. Debbie helped guide me out of this destructive thought loop and led me toward peace and understanding.

A year after Nils's death, suicidal and homicidal thoughts still arose from time to time, but were less intrusive and less frequent, and they lasted just a few moments. Over the years, I've come to accept them as part of my grieving process. They weren't pretty, and I'm not proud of them, but they're my truth, and I've learned so much about myself—and others—in the process. Nils's suicide tested the boundaries of what I was capable of and made me realize that each of us is capable of suicide or homicide under the "right" conditions. In fact, it can be a natural progression for some out of the paralysis of grief. That being said, you should *never* act on these impulses.

When I was ready to be honest about my most horrific urges and to vocalize them, I was able to receive the help I needed. If I hadn't reached out, my actions could have changed the course of my life and the lives of others. Realizing how far astray I'd gone, I was ready to pray and to focus on compassion and forgiveness. My prayers were simple: "Please remove my unkind feelings toward them," and "I pray for peace for them." Like so many survivors of suicide, I was distraught and confused, and felt I had nothing left to lose. This can be a dangerous time during the grieving process, and it's imperative that you reach out and share your feelings with someone who can help you see how destructive these thoughts are.

Spirituality, prayer, shifting my focus, and writing were key in processing my emotions. One of the principles of the 12-step process encourages "turning things over to a power greater than ourselves," and that's exactly what I did—one encounter, one flashback, and one fantasy at a time. I couldn't turn back time, but I could accept the new reality of my life, make peace with it, and acknowledge my past choices and experiences. The Serenity Prayer was helpful, too: "God, grant me the Serenity to accept the things I cannot change, the Courage to change the things I can, and the Wisdom to know the difference." It's simple yet powerful.

Anger is a natural reaction in some situations, and it helped me cope when grieving was unbearable. Sometimes it came and went swiftly; sometimes it lingered. It was also situationally directed at whoever I thought was responsible in that moment: God, Nils, the funeral director, my dad, Pierre, and others. I had created a living hell for myself by allow ing these feelings to fester. Debbie encouraged me to write about the intense feelings as a way to give them voice, which can dissipate the need to act on them. This helped enormously, and those I felt resentful toward were mostly unaware of it because of this diligent journaling practice. I also attempted to sweat it out of me through hot yoga, and studied the simple, powerful teachings of Eckhart Tolle and Tony Robbins. Eckhart believes the key is to stay in the present moment and Tony encourages shaking things up by interrupting the negative patterns.

A lot of people are afraid to share when they're mad—especially at a loved one who died. But it's normal and natural. I know this now, which is why I'm sharing what I experienced, so others don't have to suffer alone in silence. The single most important thing anyone can do when they feel vindictive is to reach out and tell a trusted confidant, which helps interrupt the pattern and return to the present moment. We're less likely to act out these feelings once they're vocalized. Their power seems to diminish when we share our truth aloud, and healing becomes more likely.

CHAPTER 6

When the Body Grieves

I thought I was having a heart attack. It felt like an elephant standing on my chest. I found it hard to breathe or catch my breath, as though every cell in my body was turning against me. I went to our family physician, and he assured me it was an anxiety attack, not a heart attack. He prescribed sleeping aids and anti-anxiety meds but given my past addictions to cocaine and prescription pills, I declined.

Part of me desperately wanted the prescriptions so I could just check out, even for a few hours, an evening, or a day. But knowing the fragility of my psychology and my addictive personality, I was afraid that in a desperate moment I might take the entire bottle and overdose, and even if I just took the sleeping pills as prescribed, the likelihood of relapse was probable, and recovery would be unlikely. I had to get through this drug-free and sober.

This was at the time my parents arrived for Nils's memorial. My body was reeling from the experience of losing Nils. I had no appetite and lost fifteen pounds in the first month. I struggled with digestion and elimination (which continued for years afterward). I didn't get my period for nine months. Grief was expressing itself through my body.

Few people talk about how traumatic grief affects us physically. My body went into shock and stopped working normally. At first, I was confused by what was happening, but soon I realized my symptoms were connected to my stress, and discovered how important physical health is to emotional healing. Bessel van der Kolk, a psychiatrist who has spent his professional life studying how children and adults adapt to traumatic experiences, wrote: "Trauma victims cannot recover until they become familiar with and befriend the sensations in their bodies. . . . Physical self-awareness is the first step in releasing the tyranny of the past."[4]

In the days, weeks, and even months after Nils died, my mind and body were processing on overload. Van der Kolk says that we can't heal and move forward as long as our bodies are still holding the trauma, and he recommends noticing and describing not just the "emotions such as frustration or anxiety or terror but the physical sensations beneath the emotions: pressure, heat, muscular tension, tingling, caving in, feeling hollow, and so on."[5] He says that when we take anti-anxiety and antidepressant drugs, we don't learn how to deal with these distressing physical reactions. Meds may give us a break, or peace, for a short time by blunting the sensations, but they do not resolve or transform these sensations into agents of healing. My mind and body needed to be reminded to *feel*, to inhabit these physical sensations and become more aware so I could better connect with myself. Although I had been trained in somatic experiencing a decade earlier and knew that physical symptoms accompany grief, it was nearly two years before I reached out for the help my body needed.

Before leaving for India with Craig, I was having a really bad time with elimination. Craig suggested I take *triphala*, an Ayurvedic remedy for digestion and elimination and consult Dr. Vasant Lad, founder of

---

[4]   Bessel A. van der Kolk, *The Body Keeps the Score: Brain, Mind, and Body in the Healing of Trauma* (New York: Viking Press, 2014), 206.

[5]   See Bessel A. van der Kolk, "Befriending the Body," on Goodreads, https://www.goodreads.com/quotes/5575683-befriending-the-body-trauma-victims-cannot-recover-until-they-become; accessed March 17, 2024.

the Ayurveda Institute in Albuquerque, New Mexico, when we got back. Ayurvedic medicine is an ancient tradition that combines herbal remedies, diet, exercise, and lifestyle changes for healing. Ayurveda, recorded more than five thousand years ago in Sanskrit in the sacred texts called the Vedas, believes that our natural state is one of health, happiness, and well-being. Health is defined as the body being clear of toxins, the mind at peace, emotions calm and happy, wastes efficiently eliminated, and organs functioning normally. In a stressful, busy, and toxic world, our physical and mental systems accumulate toxins that cause deterioration in functioning. Craig also encouraged me to do *panchakarma*, literally "five therapies," at the institute to clear my body of toxins.

So, when we returned from India, I went to Albuquerque for two weeks to receive the treatments, and I had the great fortune of attending Dr. Lad's evening lectures as well as meeting with him privately on several occasions. He told me that my *doshas*, the energies that define a person's makeup, were balanced, and that is why I survived my experience. I told him I take after my grandmother, who had a strong constitution. My gramma was my kindred spirit and the most resilient woman I've ever known. He gave me a protocol of diet and herbs and assured me I would continue to feel better. Dr. Lad is also a seer, and he helped me understand Nils's plight based on Hindu wisdom. He said I should pray for his soul, because he had created negative karma by his action.

Dr. Lad also suggested I wear an untreated white sapphire on my right index finger. White sapphire carries pure energy to balance soul and mind and bring about abundant happiness. The stone also has the ability to open our innate energy and allow it to flow. In addition, sapphire is worn for good fortune, protection, spiritual vision, and wise judgment. I was skeptical at first, but Craig encouraged me to try it, and he bought me a beautiful cushion-cut, untreated white sapphire as a gift.

When I completed the panchakarma program, I felt better physically than I had in years, and more educated about foods, herbs, and beverages to support my health and happiness. *Kitchari*, for example, is an Ayurvedic staple made of rice, split yellow mung beans, and subtle spices that are nourishing and cleansing at the same. Another example is drinking water at room temperature and eating warm, mushy food. For me, Ayurvedic medicine has been a game-changer. I always knew that what we consume affects us, but not on the cellular level I do now. And that was just one layer of my physio-emotional healing.

I had been a vegetarian on and off through my twenties and thirties. Around the time I met Craig, who was a vegetarian, I also met an American Buddhist nun, Sister Santussika, who was also a vegetarian. Thanks to their insights, I became vegetarian again, not only for physical benefits, but for soul healing as well. Sister Santussika reminded me to pray for the happiness of all beings, to honor all living things, and to practice kindness and compassion.

Kindness brings kindness, she said, especially in our bodies. Through the trauma of loss, I had forgotten to be kind to myself in ways like drinking enough liquids and getting enough rest. Sister Santussika advised me to do the things that bring me peace, wisdom, generosity, and compassion—activities that uplift the soul and help me become more mindful—including being aware of what I eat, buy, consume, and think about. My physical body, she explained, is a manifestation of what I think and do.

She encouraged me to stay present as uncomfortable feelings arose, noticing where the discomfort and depression were located in my body. She advised daily meditation, giving myself lots of space, and rest. In particular, she advised me to "Give your heart a rest." So many of us who lose loved ones feel the pain, discomfort, depression, and powerlessness in our hearts—our chest cavities. Instead of acknowledging and making peace with it, we might resist the pain and attempt to bury it, or at least cover it up for a while. We eat, work, exercise, or shop our way through it, hurting ourselves and sometimes others.

Sister Santussika felt that I couldn't find peace without acceptance, and a part of that acceptance meant (1) acknowledging my continued grief and (2) understanding that Nils is exactly where he is supposed to be. She said there's no separation between Nils and me, that we're one. His soul is always with me, she said, and it's up to me to show up for myself and for Nils each day a pure heart at peace. So, I did my best to keep my physical, mental, and emotional body pure and my karma clear.

One way to clear one's karma, she suggested, is to refrain from eating anything that has a mother. There is a lot of negative karma when ingesting an animal's karma. Most animals are not treated well before being slaughtered, and even animals that are treated well may experience anxiety, so when we ingest animals, we ingest their karma and their fear. Being a vegetarian today is rather simple and exciting with the many creative options for protein. Sister Santussika also encouraged me to spend time in the presence of what I considered holy. Her comment felt relevant, and shortly after meeting her I began visiting holy places in India, churches throughout the world, and the sea. I've always enjoyed spending time in what I consider holy, whether listening to Eckhart Tolle, David Hawkins, or Tony Robbins, or being in nature, like hiking or skiing. The one way to experience what works is to try it for thirty days or so.

Focusing on my health and well-being, I began to heal not only from the grief and trauma, but from a lifetime of mistreating my body. From the time I was thirteen and throughout my twenties, I participated in anorexic and bulimic behaviors. It started organically—watching what I ate so I'd lose weight and get thinner—and before long I was going to great lengths to radically restrict calories and eliminate certain foods. I always wore my clothes loose. I felt safe and more comfortable knowing others couldn't see my figure. I could disappear and not be seen. I felt in control. These were *my* choices; no one could take them from me. This went on for fourteen years, until things got so out of control, I went for treatment

After Nils died, I reverted to some of these behaviors, again to protect myself. I went to H&M, a women's clothing store in Geneva, and purchased an oversized pink hoodie and wore it almost all the time when I was at home. I would tuck my arms inside and pull the hood over my head to feel invisible. It brought me comfort and, again, an odd sense of control. I also began watching a lot of movies, more for refuge than entertainment. I felt physically safe because I was thrust into whatever setting I was watching, a kind of time portal. In those moments, the craziness went away. My breathing calmed and my mind got quiet. I would turn the lights off, close the drapes, lie on the couch in the den where Nils had spent his last night, and watch a film. It felt like heaven.

The oversized clothing and movies may seem inconsequential, but they brought me some relief and, in that way, contributed to my healing. What helped my mind and body become strong and healthy was having peaceful moments like those so I could be present with the uncomfortable moments and be more mindful about what I was consuming and how I was digesting life—doing things that made me feel healthy and being kind to myself and others, including animals, by becoming vegetarian again.

Healing from grief is a holistic practice. You heal your soul while healing your body, and you heal your body while healing your soul. Through awareness, loving kindness, compassion, releasing, and other holistic restorative practices, I began to find my way.

CHAPTER 7

Moving with Grace

Acceptance of the unacceptable is the greatest form of grace in this world.
— ECKHART TOLLE

M oving on" is like an abstract painting. It begins the moment we lose our loved one, and for many of us it continues for the rest of our lives. My journey began on May 8, 2011, and I'm still on it. There are times I think I'm doing great, only to feel the loss all over again. I realize now—with thirteen years behind me—that *the healing process takes time, space, and effort.*

Time helps because it creates distance from the event, but you have to take action too. You have to intentionally let go and move on. The process takes what it takes. As I discovered with sobriety, you get to embrace life one day at a time. And that's exactly what I did as I became more intimate with the grieving process.

First, I maintained good health through exercise, which I found to be integral. Nils and I exercised every day. We loved to sweat and feel our hearts beat rapidly. After he died, the idea of exercising without him seemed impossible. Doing anything that we'd enjoyed together was daunting. But I knew I had to. Self-care is foundational for healing, but knowing something and doing something about it are two different stories.

I was feeling challenged to exercise on my own. But thankfully, our dogs Quantum, a Lhasa Apso mix, and Oliver made it impossible for me to stay sedentary. They required at least a few walks a day, so I was blessed to have that motivation. I also walked for half an hour several times a week with a girlfriend who loves to walk. Walking is great for the soul. Feeling each step helped relieve my fear, anxiety, and loneliness, and after each walk, I noticed that my mood had improved. The sky looked bluer and things didn't feel quite so dark.

Eventually I returned to daily, intensive P90X workouts and running until I was exhausted. It felt great to be reengaged with P90X, because Nils and I used to enjoy these workouts together. There are twelve routines—from working on your arms to your legs to strength training to stretching, to name a few, and I still enjoy doing them. In addition, I began hiking again. Nils and I loved hiking. We loved being in nature. He took me to some of the most beautiful spots in the Swiss Alps, and we hiked by small chalets on the side of a mountain with cows grazing in the meadows. In addition, I continued care for our garden, removing pesky weeds, pruning trees, and raking fallen leaves. The physicality helped me touch the many knowns and unknowns of my life. Gardening became a metaphor for my life—powerful and grounding.

An unexpected gift came to me in Dubai—hot yoga!—and it's still a sacred practice for me. One afternoon in mid-September 2011, I felt I was unraveling and thought that I might need to be admitted to a psychiatric unit. I called Debbie, and she felt I would benefit from a change of scenery to distance myself from the stress and craziness around Nils's estate. Nils and I had spent a lot of time in Dubai over the years, so I flew there and stayed with a friend for a few weeks. One day without explanation, she told me to drink two liters of water and put on a T-shirt and shorts. Off we went to a Bikram Yoga studio.

Upon arrival, the instructor asked me to commit to staying in the room while keeping my eyes open no matter what, and I agreed. The heat, the poses, the effort of matching my breath to movement, were overwhelming—and instantly transformative. For ninety minutes, I felt as though I were in a womb—suspended from time, safe, whole, and present. There was something powerfully painful about doing the twenty-six poses twice each, while silently releasing the toxins and emotions that had been building up in me. When the instructor led us into camel pose, which is a heart opener, she warned that it might be an emotional experience and to let the energies flow freely. Tears were rolling down my cheeks as I could feel the energy rushing through my heart. As my heart opened, the love I felt for Nils flowed. The camel pose still has that effect on me. I'm always excited to walk into a hot yoga studio and place my mat and water on the floor. It is a coming-home ritual for me.

It's also incredibly grounding. As I get into *savasana*, the corpse pose, my focus is on relaxing and breathing in and out of my nose, conscious of every breath. Breathing pulls me into the present moment—out of my mind and into my body. We live so much of the time in our heads. Hot yoga helps quiet the overactive mind. Often at the beginning of a yoga class, my interactions and activities that day flash by like a short film. But during hot yoga, they seem to dissipate because of the breathing, the heat, and the power of the poses. In each session, my mind gets still. I surrender to the experience and walk away feeling great, knowing something has been released, a deep sense of a peaceful accomplishment that I honored my body and soul. Most important, I know I'll be able to take the peace and coherence I feel during those ninety minutes back into the world with me.

In addition to physical movement and exercise, I continued to attend 12-step support-group meetings several times a week. These were important times for me to socialize, feel connected to the world around me, and be reminded of the primacy of staying sober and helping others who may be struggling. From day one, I knew I'd be candid about how Nils died and how I was doing. It was important for me to share my experiences, strengths, and hopes, and to affirm that regardless of how quickly changes were occurring and how uncomfortable these changes might be, I was determined to stay sober and take responsibility for how I show up in the world.

I was doing more things on my own now, which was an adjustment: For three and a half gorgeous years, Nils and I had spent almost every day together. Getting out of the house, interacting with others, and reaching out for encouragement were vital to moving on. It's important to find a support group that resonates with you. No one can go through such a trauma alone. And you'll be surprised how willing others are to help, even those you might not have expected to care.

Allowing myself to be open to receiving support, kindness, and encouragement was important, but I knew that *giving* love, support, and encouragement to others was even more integral to my stability and healing, if not my survival. Serving others, I was able to get out of myself and focus on them. I cleaned up after meetings, often went to dinner afterward, and made "we care" calls to other members. I became available to my sponsees and resumed my responsibilities as the area chair for the English-speaking 12-step fellowship in Geneva and the surrounding cantons.

I also started helping at the Salvation Army's soup kitchen, quickly committing to three meals a week. Spontaneous tears would roll down my cheeks as I was serving others or washing their dishes. Those receiving the free meals just smiled at me. It helped me feel I mattered and helped me remember that others were suffering, too. I looked forward to being there, because I was making a difference in someone's life, and they were making a difference in mine. I became fond of many of the regulars; we seemed to brighten each other's days, even for a moment. Despite the language barrier, my supervisor was very supportive and gave me the space to be wherever I was emotionally.

And I also got involved with the International Committee of the Red Cross, whose world headquarters are in Geneva. I was able to work as a volunteer in the archives department. This, too, helped me shift my focus and attention to others, even just four hours a week. My supervisor was patient while I'd mumble to myself, have poor concentration, and sometimes just weep. He simply encouraged me and was always as happy to see me as I was to see him.

The 12-step fellowship has traditions that govern the integrity of the groups. The tradition that helped me the most through this period was tradition 1, "Our common welfare should come first." I did my best, one day at a time, to make being of service a priority while honoring the traditions in my daily life. I'm super grateful I have this knowing about service, because it kept me from becoming self-absorbed, which would only have led to a "poor me" state of mind, hindered the healing process, and served no one.

Getting more actively involved in my community, I began to feel more useful—I could make a difference even when I wasn't in the best of shape. It didn't seem to matter that I spoke only a little French. I was able to make a difference just by showing up. And these people and institutions helped save my life, reinforcing that I mattered and was loved.

My parents and my brother were happy that I was finding my way but encouraged me to come back to the States to welcome the New Year with them. Even though I'd be leaving Switzerland for just a month, I had some trepidation leaving Nils. At the same time, I loved the hustle and bustle of Christmas shopping, beautiful decorations, and light displays of Christmas in the US. I had no idea how important it would be for my spirit. My itinerary included Port Angeles, Washington; Santa Monica; and Miami, Florida.

In early December 2011, just seven months after Nils's passing, Pierre took me to the Geneva Airport. I was immediately reminded of the wonderful times Nils and I had had while traveling. The passport control officer asked why I was tearing up, and I told him, "I'm missing my dead husband." He smiled and told me, "My wife died eleven years ago and I still miss her terribly." When I boarded my flight to Frankfurt, the seat next to me was empty and I could feel Nils's presence there, encouraging me to enjoy my life. As we were flying above the clouds, I noticed a beautiful rainbow that seemed to be following our plane. I spent half an hour talking to Nils and envisioning him flying around in his own private plane acting like the mischievous six-year-old I had come to love. He was very much alive, and I assured him that I wouldn't harm myself. I encouraged him to fly to the destinations he always wanted to see, to be happy, to keep an eye on me, and to show me a sign from time to time that he was with me. It was liberating to be flying on my own.

My first stop was Port Angeles, to visit my uncle and my ninety-one-year-old grandmother for a few weeks. He could take some time off, and I would look after her. Gramma and I laughed a lot and cried about her husband's death and Nils's death. My grandmother had been told Nils had a heart attack. She asked me what happened and said, "Don't lie to me." I burst into tears and told her the truth, and she wrapped her arms around me. She then proceeded to call him an asshole. She adored Nils. She reminded me of when Nils and I surprised her on her ninetieth birthday. We flew from Geneva to Seattle on January 24, 2011. Her kids had planned a surprise party, which meant a lot of relatives and friends would be coming to town. Nils loved my gramma, and we decided to keep our arrival a secret. When we arrived, she was still sleeping. Nils and I stood above her and gently woke her. She burst into tears when she saw us. She grabbed us, gave us both big hugs, said, "Wow! I was worth your traveling all this way."

Nils and I both began to cry. The simple gesture of us flying across the Atlantic brought her so much joy. She understood how important she was to us. Before leaving Washington State, we took her to her favorite Jack in the Box for a monster taco and loaded her up with dark chocolate. She talked about this now as if it had just happened and promised when she sees Nils in heaven, she'll give him a talkin' to and a huge hug. I just love my grandmother!

Throughout my visit, I became her nurse, which required a lot of focus because she had many morning and evening medications, eye-drops, and so on. She sent me on a mission to buy dark chocolate at the local "Wally World" (her nickname for Walmart). Most importantly, we spent time reminiscing about her life. What struck me most was that she didn't share any stories of regret or resentment. She'd had a rather tough life—raising six kids with little money and enduring my grandpa's abuse when he'd been drinking. Her stories were filled with love, laughter, sweetness, compassion, and gratitude. My grandmother has always been a kindred spirit and one of the most important and influential women in my life. I left knowing that she knew how much I loved, admired, respected, and thought of her. My heart was filled with joy and gratitude when I said goodbye, not knowing when I would see her again.

Another highlight before leaving Port Angeles was a visit to a nearby corrections facility with a longtime member of the 12-step fellowship. The atmosphere was intimidating. We were met by armed guards, and we told them we were there to take part in the weekly 12-step meeting. We were escorted through half a dozen locked doors until approximately twenty men of all races, ranging in age from eighteen to sixty, greeted us. I introduced myself, shook hands with each of them, and told them how grateful I was to be there. A few of the younger men seemed restless and were a bit disruptive, which I found challenging. After a couple of them shared their stories, I shared mine. The room became quiet. None of these guys had ever come home to find a loved one hanging in their garage. My message was simple and clear: Left untreated, addiction destroys lives and kills. No matter what is going on in your life, choose to stay sober—refrain from taking a substance to make you feel better. You could hear a pin drop.

There was a lot of honest sharing. Many were lifers with no possibility of parole. Several had sixty-year sentences, and some were young gang-bangers doing their best to find their way. While our backgrounds were entirely different, we had a lot in common. The difference between most of them and me was that I had never gotten arrested for the crimes I committed when I was using. I was fortunate to have never maimed or killed someone while driving under the influence. Most of them had been incarcerated because of crimes they committed while under the influence.

I have great compassion for the men I met that day. In many ways, meeting with them changed my life. It deepened my appreciation of freedom, something many of us take for granted. And it made me realize I have a second chance at life. Nils didn't get one. These men didn't get one, at least not yet. They were behind bars for their drug or alcohol use. They did, however, have the opportunity to get and stay sober and to share their message with their loved ones, the guards, and people like me who had the good fortune of meeting them. On some level, they did have a second chance. My experience that day instilled in me a deep and abiding sense of gratitude, realizing how fortunate I am to be alive and free. And I felt on a visceral level an obligation to Nils—and to these men—to make the most of my second chance and live the best life I can.

Family relationships can be an important part of healing, one that is sometimes overlooked. After Port Angeles, I went to Santa Monica for a few days and stayed with my dad. One evening my mom and I went to see my aunt Lucy, whose son died in a car accident. We made her dinner and chatted for hours. It was the first time I had seen her since Tyler's death, and still, we laughed and cried and reminisced about life and death. It was a beautiful evening filled with a sweet spirit of love, laughter, forgiveness, and tears. I left feeling a deep connection with her and a heart filled with gratitude. It was as though we'd never lost contact even though we hadn't spoken in nearly twenty years. She understood the deep pain and sorrow, and the steps required to move forward after the sudden tragic loss of someone you love. It was quite extraordinary that Nils's death created an opening for my aunt Lucy and me to share honestly about her journey, about Tyler, and about my late husband she'd never met.

It's always fun to be at my dad's house around the holidays, because his neighbors go to great lengths to decorate their homes. Many of them work in the movie industry, and their displays are out of this world. One front lawn was set up like Santa's toy shop with lifelike elves and reindeers galore, and an imitation snow machine. It was a beautiful time of year to be there; seeing the many festive displays boosted my spirits. My parents, quite concerned about my well-being, encouraged me to move back to the US, but I was not ready yet.

The final stop was Miami, to visit my brother and his four kids. I had the good fortune to meet my five-month-old niece, Violet, who was born in July 2011 (just two months after Nils's passing), and to see my two-year-old nephew, James, who I barely knew. James wanted to learn to swim, and I got to teach him. This kid had the courage and passion of a tiger. Watching his eyes light up as he grinned from ear to ear each time he jumped into the pool was just awesome. His enthusiasm was as strong on his thirtieth jump as on his first.

I also spent time with my niece, Maggie, and turned her on to a movie called *D.E.B.S.*, which we watched every night before going to sleep. And each night it was like watching it for the first time. Her enthusiasm for day-to-day stuff was inspiring. One night before we went to sleep, she rolled over and said, "I love you, Auntie Kim." *Wow! What a moment!* I also enjoyed spending time at the beach with Zane, my oldest nephew and the quietest of them all. I missed Nils's children so much and had treasured our nighttime routine. Now, with my brother's children, I was able to appreciate how blessed I was to have been a stepparent, even for just a few years. Being with children again was exactly what I needed to mend my broken heart.

One evening I was in the kitchen and decided to play one of Charlie and Clara's favorite songs by Alvin and the Chipmunks, "Witch Doctor." Zane, Maggie, and James came running into the kitchen, and as we laughed and danced, I felt tears welling up in my eyes, expressing the sheer joy of being an auntie and wanting to contribute to them having a little more fun. Kids have a way of bringing you down to earth and keeping you in the present moment. I love my nieces and nephews and will carry these beautiful memories with me always. Spending time with young children is incredibly soulful—and a reminder of the precious, ephemeral nature of life.

One morning toward the end of my stay in Miami, I woke up early to go for a jog. There was a slight breeze and pouring rain as the dawn was beginning to break. I was totally present; it was amazing. My mind was still. I was simply enjoying each step, each raindrop, each person and each boat I passed. I felt connected to the universe. I stopped and sat quietly on a bench, feeling the pouring rain on my face. It was a cleanse, or a clearing.

The trip to America helped me in so many ways. My adventures distracted me from feeling depressed because my spirit was flooded with pleasurable moments. I was surrounded by my family who, for the most part, were enjoying their lives. The individual moments and the totality of the journey became treasured memories. I was able to connect with more laughter, gratitude, wonder, reconciliation, beauty, acceptance, and even letting go. To think I would have missed all these precious moments if I had harmed myself or someone else or had not stayed sober after Nils's passing. I could see how important it was for me to keep having new and different experiences. Forcing myself to engage in life was one of the most powerful acts of healing I experienced and a wonderful way to honor Nils.

Exhilaration had been essential for Nils. His determined spirit shone through at an early age. He told me about the first marathon he ran when he was fourteen. He and his friend decided they needed new running shoes, and they managed to get Nike to sponsor them! They ran the marathon together in a T-shirt built for two with "Nike" written boldly across their chests. Their efforts made the Swedish papers. He also dreamed of skiing, but his parents always took the family to sunny vacation spots in winter. So Nils spent hours on his own studying how and where to ski and the kinds of equipment needed. Finally, at age eighteen, he got to ski, and he fell in love with it instantly. He loved that it required guts. Skiing down a steep slope creates an adrenaline-rush and some fear, which forced him to master his emotions. He loved the smell of the crisp mountain air, the feel of the powder under his skis, and that each run was different depending on the skier's mood, health, the weather, and the condition of the mountain. He loved the the performance gear that assisted him in skiing his best, and spending time in the chalet. He loved gathering the wood and placing it carefully in the fireplace. He loved the sounds of the logs crackling and the warmth and ambiance it created for us all. His face lit up every time he shared these stories.

Nils went to great lengths to support his children having new experiences, too. He moved them when they were young from Sweden to a more international and open-minded country. While in Switzerland exploring where they might reside, he went for a run by Lake Geneva and through Geneva's *vieille-ville* ("old town"), a maze of picturesque streets filled with cafés, restaurants, museums, and historical sights. In the center of the district, he saw a majestic carousel filled with kids and the sounds of laughter, and that sealed the deal. He knew this community would be supportive of children, which was a priority for him.

Nils loved traveling and experiencing new cultures. He loved sampling new coffees. He loved listening to a variety of styles of music. I often asked him to dance with me, and he would get up and make some wild moves, like John Travolta in *Saturday Night Fever*, but politely declined slow dancing. He didn't feel qualified. There is something intimate associated with slow dancing, about which he felt some discomfort. However, he loved tinkering on the piano and guitar and could play both instruments by ear. He loved telemark skiing and wanted his children to be great skiers too. He loved watching movies. He spoke Swedish, French, English, and Russian fluently and was learning Arabic. Unlike the other languages, Russian was difficult for him, and he was proud that he'd applied himself and learned how to speak it fluently in just a few years. He loved challenges.

Despite his wealth and appreciation of the "finer things," he enjoyed simplicity—wearing jeans from the Gap, taking walks, spending time with his kids, and doing things for the pure joy of it. When we were in New York, we volunteered for One Brick, a community of volunteers who support local nonprofits. We got to paint an elementary school cafeteria in the Bronx and stuffed fundraising envelopes to support a South African youth program, to name just a few projects we thoroughly enjoyed. Even though Nils went reluctantly at first, he came to love helping out. He also was generous, supporting charities financially. I'm grateful for Nils's openness and curiosity.

Step by step, movement by movement, experience by experience, one day at a time, I noticed that I was moving with *Grace*. Grace was always there, but now I was able to be more present with it—less attached to the past, less anxious about the future, connecting deeply to each moment. I continue to embrace new experiences for the sheer joy of it.

In early 2014, I began playing tennis. Having a sport during which I could *hit* something helped ease my angst and diminish the sadness that was still popping up. I often hit tennis balls with a friend, so we both got some exercise and a chance to catch up. More recently, I've taken up golf. It's incredibly challenging and requires you to sustain your focus and commit to every shot while letting go as you swing the club, which feels counterintuitive. I love that you can play alone or just go to the driving range. It's also fun playing different courses and enjoying the unique beauty of each, including the sand traps and water hazards. I feel blessed because our friends Dave and Frances love to play golf with Craig and me. I also feel fortunate I get to play with Craig, who normally doesn't like to engage in sports with women. For me, golf embodies Nils's philosophy about experiences—a joyful celebration of health and life. I feel a part of the tennis community and am becoming a part of the golf community.

It's so important in the healing process to take up new activities and create entirely new experiences not associated with the past. Craig loves scuba diving and encouraged me to give it a try. I love the way partners and friends can encourage us to do things we might not do on our own. I was extremely anxious at first because of the movie *Jaws*, which I saw when I was thirteen. However, I embraced my fear and took that leap of faith off the boat and was surprised by the restorative benefits. Diving deep into the sea is an intense and extraordinary experience and a reminder of how tiny we are in comparison to the ocean. Sea life is a visual reminder of our own beauty, grace, strength, and need for one another. It's breathtaking to bear witness to the magnificence of sea creatures in glorious detail—and their differences and similarities—not to mention our own similarities to them. The sound of my breathing via the regulator is like a meditation. It helps me stay relaxed, cognizant of my dive buddy, and my surroundings. Being immersed in the sea also invigorates and rejuvenates my body. It helps reduce anxiety and stress in the body because the salt water reduces cortisol levels. I can literally feel my entire being more integrated and more peaceful when I complete a dive.

In 2020 during a dive trip in Bora Bora, Tahiti, at about twenty feet deep, our divemaster, Craig, and I came upon a formation of gorgeous eagle rays. It was breathtaking to watch these magnificent creatures as if suspended in motion—as if remaining still—in front of us, despite their graceful efforts to move forward in the current. It seemed magical and mystical. We were all in the same current, moving steadily an inch at a time in the direction we wanted to go. We were all exactly where we should have been, taking all the time we needed. Grief is like that. It may feel like we're making no progress, as though we're suspended, stuck against a powerful and forceful current that threatens to carry us away at each moment; but if we keep swimming, slowly, gracefully, consistently, we will move forward—a day, an inch, a moment at a time, like the eagle rays.

CHAPTER 8

Letting Go

Purification is the act of letting go. This is done out of discriminative awareness.
That is, you understand that you are an entity passing through
a life in which the entire drama is an
offering for your awakening.
— RAM DASS

D espite my successes moving forward, grief remained a strong current in my life. At one point, I realized I was holding on to too much
from the past, and if I wanted to progress, I needed to surrender and let go
of beliefs and things that were holding me back—wanting to return to
what could never be again—and to face an uncertain future. Letting Nils
go, not to mention the incredible life we shared, was extremely challenging.

Craig and I had the great fortune of attending several annual "Open
Your Heart in Paradise" retreats on Maui led by Ram Dass and others,
including Sharon Salzberg, Krishna Das, Trudy Goodman, and Jack
Kornfield. I love Ram Dass's wit and contagious smile, and continue to
learn from him, even since his passing in late 2019. During one retreat,
he and others were discussing death—not only how we approach our
own death but also how we grieve the loss of loved ones; and Ram Dass
encouraged us to do so consciously. In the West, we are eager to make
uncomfortable feelings go away: "Just give me something to take the
edge off," we might say when we're anxious or in pain. We want to be
numbed. If we don't take drugs or alcohol, we may seek other distrac-
tions, hoping the discomfort will disappear.

Another way we approach grief is to "work it out," "understand it," or "get to the bottom of it" through talk therapy. Ram Dass didn't think this was always effective, although for some it can be. He suggested, instead, to give our grief process the space to run its course. We're not only grieving a physical loss, but the dreams and desires associated with the one who has died. He advised us to "let it go," that our attachments to the past, the future, or even to "reasons" for our suffering often create more suffering. Our minds judge what happened, and self-blame and blaming others are endless. Ram Dass called suffering "fierce grace."

His statements resonated within me. Within days of Nils's suicide, someone suggested I meet with a psychologist to talk about my feelings, to get at the "source of it." I was still in shock and could barely speak, let alone understand how or why I was feeling what I was feeling, so the session was brief. But I was determined not to take any mind-altering substances, prescribed or not.

In the West, our approach to grief and death often lacks a spiritual component, or even an acknowledgment of the *reality* of our own mortality. When death comes knocking on our door or at the door of a loved one, we may be shocked. I certainly was. Yet this is the deal: "We are all in the queue," as the Buddhist teacher Sharon Salzberg says. Not one of us is getting out of this alive, and yet we walk around thinking we're invulnerable. And because some don't acknowledge their own mortality, death can have a devastating effect on us. The sooner we accept the inevitability of our own death and the death of others and learn to *let go*, the sooner we become free.

I knew I needed to look at physical death and the death of our marriage squarely and with courage. I wanted to embrace it all, gracefully when possible and not so gracefully when necessary. Letting go and accepting death are monumental tasks, and to do so, I had to let go of Nils *incrementally*. It was not going to happen overnight, but for me to thrive, which is what Nils would have wanted, I needed to take these necessary though challenging steps.

Nils's Celebration of Life was ten days after his passing. We decided to have it at our home so that those coming could enjoy the beauty of being outdoors, enjoy the pool, play table tennis, or just be. His two sisters, their husbands, and their children had arrived from Sweden the night before.

It proved to be a peaceful yet frenetic day. I wanted to be of service to Nils and his family and friends who loved him. His nieces and nephews from Sweden made a lovely welcome sign in Swedish, English, and French, and taped it to the front gate. I spontaneously wrote a description of him on a fifteen-foot piece of art paper and hung it on the kitchen wall. In fact, it would have taken a sheet of paper the length of Switzerland to express it all.

Our home was filled with the sounds of children laughing, splashing in the pool, and playing with Chili, the kids' dog, Oliver, and Quantum. There were also family and friends sharing beautiful memories of Nils, telling stories about their adventures with him, some hilarious. Some folks just sat quietly and wept. The house was both eerily quiet and very much alive. I did my best to focus on Nils's kids. They were missing their papa and were as confused and bewildered as I was. Needing to be near him and alone, I later found myself seeking comfort at the foot of our walk-in closet once again. I wrapped myself in the workout outfit he'd worn the day before he died. It still smelled like him. I drifted asleep and was gently awakened by my mom encouraging me to come back downstairs.

Raushana had put together a beautiful slide show with photos of Nils, his family, and his friends, and people stood and watched. There was lots of great food, and the sound of a ping-pong ball being hit, honoring how much Nils enjoyed playing table tennis. Before people left, we formed a circle so those who wanted to share could, while Nils's friend Tim played his guitar ever so gently. Tim had had conversations with Nils about their mutual belief in parallel universes. Tim had jokingly cautioned Nils that he did not want to come home one day to find him in his apartment. He reminded the kids and me how much Nils spoke about us and how much he loved us.

Nils's youngest sister recited a beautiful short poem and expressed her deep love and admiration for her brother. Anna-Mae, a friend of Nils, thanked him for his consistent kindness and generosity over the

Nils

Lived passionately

Loved with his whole heart

Enjoyed beating people at table tennis

Loved playing football with Charlie and watching him play on a team

Loved being cuddled

Adored high-tech things, especially big flat-screen TVs, Apple products, and cool gadgets

Enjoyed watching movies and discovering and listening to the latest bands

Absolutely loved listening to the State Capella of St. Petersburg (Russia) Choir

Loved wearing blue jeans, T-shirts, and lots of Jo Malone cologne

Loved laughing and telling jokes

Fanatical about P90X and telemark skiing

Extremely competitive and got a lot of pleasure outrunning me

Loved spending time in the mountains and chalets

Had a resourceful, adventurous, and creative soul

Enjoyed watching Clara take swimming lessons at our local gym

Had the courage of a warrior

Was fascinated by languages and mastering difficult ones like Russian

Loved living in New York and walking its busy streets

Loved helping Emma with her homework

Enjoyed intense conversations with his friend Pierre

An incredible debater about topics he was passionate about

Loved our home filled with the sounds of his children's laughter, dogs barking—
and my American way of being

A genius

Deeply loved his parents, sisters, brothers-in-law, nieces, and nephews

Loved downloading music with Mia

Was an amazing husband who assisted me in seeing my physical beauty

Was a great friend to many and contributed to the world being a better place

Was a complicated yet simple being

The world has lost an extraordinary person. We all love you and miss you very, very much.

Loving you, Kimberly

years. My dad, although crying, was able to express his gratitude to Nils for making me so happy and his own love and admiration for Nils. Many people wept quietly.

Tim continued strumming Nils's guitar throughout the Celebration of Life. He knew how much Nils loved to play the guitar. I was staring at Tim when he looked up at me gently and began singing "Woman in Red." Tears streamed down my face. Nils used to sing that song to me while playing the guitar, even though I had never owned a red dress. Tim stopped abruptly, and for a few minutes there was silence. People just looked at one another, some smiling, some crying, some expressionless, and some seeming lost. I softly reminded his children how much their papa loved each of them and that I knew how deeply sorry he was for creating so much suffering. At that moment, Tim resumed playing guitar and singing the closing verses of the song. The words and Tim's gaze went right through me. Tears welled up in his eyes as he strummed Nils's guitar for the last time.

The following day, I had to let his last physical remnants go. Nils had told me clearly that he wanted his ashes scattered on his beloved Mont Blanc in Chamonix, in the French Alps where he skied and spent so much time with his family. Charlie, Clara, Mia, Emma, his ex-wife, my stepmom, my parents, and I left with Nils's ashes for Chamonix in the early afternoon. In a little over an hour we were in the village and boarded the Aiguille du Midi *télécabine* to one of his favorite slopes on Mont Blanc to release the ashes. The finality of the burial of a loved one can be both heart-rending and celebratory. Like so many who lose loved ones, I struggled when the time came to let him go.

It was overcast when we boarded the cable car silently. The ride up felt like eternity. We just stared at one another. Nils was still in a Ziploc bag tucked in the sparkly blue box, which I held tightly in my hands. It would be the last time I'd physically hold him. The other people on the cable car were enthusiastic about being on Mont Blanc, excited about the beauty of the area. I could almost hear Nils whispering similar sentiments.

Once we reached the top, we had to decide where to leave him. We walked down to a slope Nils skied every winter and decided on a place where a boulder would provide some shelter. I placed the bright blue box on a large flat rock, took off the top, and opened the Ziploc bag. Each of us just stared at Nils and then at each other. He was now ashes—coarse and gritty in texture and a pasty, light gray in color. We didn't really know what to do next. It was a situation none of us was equipped to handle.

Mia and I burst into tears and held each other's hands. Then Clara looked at me with her beautiful eyes and suggested we each take a handful of Papa's ashes and scatter them on the mountain. It was the perfect thing to do, because it was a physical way of being close to Nils one last time. We took turns taking handfuls of Nils and throwing him on the mountain while shouting and whispering things, each of us grieving in our own way. I said, "I love you; I will miss you, and keep an eye on me until we meet again. . . ."

The mountains echoed with our Swedish and English sentiments. Though holding Nils's ashes in my hand helped me see *and feel* the finality of it all, I also knew this was only the beginning. I felt torn apart—part of me wanted to hold on to him forever and another part knew he didn't *belong* to me. Now he was where he loved to be, and a rush of serenity flooded my body. It felt like he was home and no longer suffering. At the same time, I was suffering terribly, as were his family and friends.

Everyone else went up to a small café that overlooked the slope where Nils was now a part of something bigger than himself, and I decided to stay a while and have a chat with him. Overwhelmed with emotion, I fell to my knees and begged the universe to help his children and me through this nightmare. Needing to be near him, I lay there for half an hour, feeling the mountain on my back, listening to his favorite songs on my iPhone. It was so quiet, even with his music playing. I was startled when my phone began ringing, and grabbed it thinking it was Nils calling to let me know he was on his way home and that this had all been a big misunderstanding. Of course, it wasn't. But it felt like a miracle. There was no cell service where we were, but for some reason in that moment my phone rang. There was no one on the line, so I took it as a sign he would be okay and was now being looked after by nature—the birds, the sky, the trees, and the mountain.

An hour earlier, Nils had been near me in a blue box, and now he was completely gone, scattered on Mont Blanc. He was dust and a part of the mountain he loved so much. Covering all the bases, I asked God to take care of Nils's spirit, to guide and love his children as they learned to navigate life without their papa's guidance. Before leaving the mountain, I took off a small gold bracelet Nils had bought for me in Dubai and buried it in the earth. I didn't want him feeling alone and afraid, so I thought if I left a part of me on the slope, he wouldn't feel abandoned.

My parents stepped out of the café and called down asking me to join them. My heart wanted to set up a tent and never leave this sacred spot. As I walked up to join the others, I felt a breeze rush through my body, as though Nils were giving me a hug. When I arrived, everyone was in the small chalet having a drink and sitting quietly. Mia came up to me, placed a beautiful amethyst stone in the palm of my hand, and with tears streaming down her face, hugged me and said, "Papa loved you so much." I wiped the tears from her face, gave her a warm hug, and reminded her how much I loved her but most importantly how much her papa had loved her. As we walked back to the cable car, Nils's ex-wife grabbed my hand and said, "Thank you for all that you have done." She expressed her thankfulness for being included in the memorial service the day before and the experience we'd just shared. I felt like we were going to muddle through this experience united, which brought me some comfort. It wasn't until a few weeks later that I received the news that all contact with my stepkids would be severed.

The drive home was quiet. We were all digesting what we had experienced. I was devastated by no longer having Nils near, and at the same time, I felt peaceful that his ashes were *home*. He'd always called himself a mountain boy, and he was finally in the place that had brought him so much joy. When I returned to our house later that afternoon, the energy there had changed; Nils was no longer in the sparkly bright blue box on his desk.

I didn't think there was anything left to let go of, that I had lost it all, already. But life has a way of showing us just how much more there is inside of us to grieve and release. Shortly after Nils's death and the children's departure, I was determined to hold on to the people, places, and things Nils and I had shared together, believing this was a way to stay connected to him and keep his memory alive.

When Nils was alive, I felt like Cinderella every day, though my foot slipped into a sneaker rather than a glass slipper. He was always surprising me, loving me, and taking me on adventures that enriched my life with excitement, beauty, love, and growth. I was in love with my life, in love with the people in it, and felt I was exactly where I was supposed to be. There were a few brief moments in the early days of our courtship when I thought this extraordinary experience would vanish, like Cinderella's stagecoach that turned back into a pumpkin and her stagecoach men became mice. So, when it all vanished, I felt certain I had failed in my spiritual practice, like not being grateful enough or not setting powerful enough intentions. It dawned on me later that those closest to Nils, like me, must have also felt some responsibility for his action, even though Nils was the primary actor. Letting go of self-flagellation can be a monumental task.

Nils shared his enthusiasm for anything electronic. He bought me my first iPhone and MacBook laptop, which I still use to this day, and he introduced me to flying privately through NetJets, and ultimately on his own after he bought a plane, which had been, for him, a childhood dream. He had the Swedish and American flags painted on the tail. He was so incredibly proud of getting his pilot's license and owning a plane. He asked me to manage the aircraft despite my total unfamiliarity with airplane management or maintenance. I learned quickly that safety standards and requirements for aircraft were more lenient in Europe than in the US. It was challenging, rewarding, and fun, all at the same time, to learn about the aviation industry.

He was also proud that he owned a home in America, a luxury

condo in the Plaza Residences overlooking Central Park, where we lived part time. He said he wasn't much of a real estate guy, but the real estate he owned was always in a prime location. Nils loved the hustle and bustle of the city. The intense energy of New York was calming for him. We loved walking the busy streets together, taking subways, strolling, and running through Central Park.

We often watched the TV show *The Dog Whisperer* with Cesar Millan. I was impressed by how Cesar worked with the owners and rehabilitated the dogs. I loved that he understood energy. Nils just thought it was good entertainment. One afternoon while walking up 59th Street, we walked directly into him while he was waiting for a cab outside the Helmsley Hotel. I grabbed Nils, and we stopped right in front of Cesar while I told him how much I loved his show. I asked him to explain energy to Nils, and said that we had several dogs, as though we were the only ones on this busy street. Cesar was generous with us, offering us a precious ten minutes of his time and expertise.

Nils loved having a doorman at our building to greet him every time he walked in and out, and someone at the front desk to help with groceries and errands. We also loved getting up at 4:00 each morning when we were in New York. Because of the time differences with Europe and Russia, that's when Nils would start working. After the sun rose, we shared our appreciation for the gorgeous view of the park, regardless of the time of day or season. We often sat by the window with our cups of coffee expressing deep gratitude for being alive and having the incredible fortune of living in this historic building. He enjoyed being pampered, and it was pretty amazing for me as well. For a brief time, I lived the life of a fairy tale.

Nils, the kids, and I spent summer vacations in New York, Florida, and California. On our first trip to California, his kids got to meet my parents. We stayed at my mother's house, because Nils thought it would be nice for them to get to know her. We all loved the beaches, especially the craziness of the Venice boardwalk with clowns on roller skates, street artists, and hippies in every manner of attire. The kids were mesmerized by the thrilling rides at Magic Mountain amusement park, and the girls enjoyed clothes shopping at Macy's and even put on a fashion show for my mom. Nils loved my mother and insisted she fly back to Switzerland with us. He wanted to surprise her because we were flying home on a Gulfstream private jet. When we arrived at one of the private airports near LAX, Nils walked her to the tall window overlooking the tarmac, pointed to our plane, and explained that we could board at any time. She was speechless. It was a night flight, but she stayed up all night needlepointing, being pampered by the stewardess, and thoroughly loving the experience. Doing this brought Nils so much happiness; he loved uplifting others.

We spent winters skiing in Megève and Chamonix, in France, on some of the best ski slopes in the world. Perhaps our happiest memories, though, were on Mont Blanc, although it was never easy to get the kids dressed and out into the cold. Despite momentary complaints, we all enjoyed those glorious times in the two-story wooden chalet with a heated swimming pool, where we could hang out after long days on the slopes. Emma, Mia, and Clara would glide down the mountain with ease, so quickly it was hard for me to keep up with them. So I often skied with Charlie. On the slopes, Nils was in heaven. He just radiated, truly a mountain boy.

Back in the chalet, we laughed a lot, ate a bunch, and watched movies. When I think of those times—all the laughter and happiness—I feel a mix of sadness and immense joy. I miss it a lot and realize I can never replicate those precious and priceless moments with Nils and his children. I also feel intensely thankful that Nils chose as his final resting place Mont Blanc, where many of his happiest moments remain. We'll be able to look at Mont Blanc and see him, feel him, and know he's there, in the air, the sunshine, and the snow, watching over and loving us.

When I visited New York after Nils passed, I was reminded of his excitement when we experienced Manhattan with his kids. Seeing the world through their eyes—their wonder and awe—was a gift to us both. Everything seemed so big and so beautiful. As we walked through Central Park, we watched the kids' eyes become the size of silver dollars. They were amazed by the enormity of the buildings, the sounds of the taxis, and the people hustling about. They enjoyed buying hot dogs from street vendors and taking the subway to the movie theater.

Nils went to the movies with Emma and Mia, while Clara, Charlie, and I would do something more for the little ones. One afternoon, Emma, fifteen years old, and I took the subway to Herald Square. I went to exchange a pair of sandals, but really I wanted to spend some time alone with Emma. I thought she might enjoy visiting a store filled just with women's shoes. As we walked through the doors, she was speechless. *Shoes everywhere, of every color and height!* As I tried on different sized sandals, she tried on a pair of four-inch heels, smiling from ear to ear. I couldn't resist taking a photo of her so she could show her girlfriends back home. She said, "I can't wait to show Papa." It was exciting experiencing New York with them and sharing the beautiful apartment Nils and I had created.

When I first returned to New York—or anywhere Nils and I had been together—I was torn. I wanted to remember and at the same time, it *hurt* to remember. I wondered, as so many people do after the sudden loss of a loved one—*Will I ever be able to look back on the happy memories and smile—and not feel the pain of their absence?* The answer is absolutely yes, and it begins when we're able to face the memories, be grateful for them, and thank them for being wonderful teachers. We can learn not to judge those memories as good or bad, painful or happy, but as moments in time that brought us closer to awareness. It's a continuous process.

Spending time in places that had been sacred to us, with all the memories, contributed to my feeling that Nils was deeply present and alive inside me. We spent so much time together laughing, enjoying each other's company, and celebrating life. Even without ski trips to Mont Blanc or visits to New York aboard a private jet, our life would have been wonderful. Nils didn't need to do extravagant things to keep me happy, he just needed to be himself. Some of our greatest moments were snuggling at home on an Ikea couch watching movies together—and we could have done that anywhere.

*   *   *

Letting go of our loved ones, and even their pets and their possessions, is a process. You have to take it one step at a time. I knew that relocating to the United States was inevitable, but it was unclear how long I should stay in Switzerland. I couldn't bring myself to leave quite yet. I felt that if I didn't stay there, I would lose all contact with Nils. I was still holding on to a belief that none of this was true. Letting go meant moving from the places and things he and I once loved together. Once I was able to understand this, I became open to moving back to the US.

The first step was to move from our home in Collonge-Bellerive, where I had become emotionally attached to him. But before I could, I had to decide what to do with Oliver. We all loved Nils's dog Oliver, but he was never the same after Nils died. He looked lost and often ran around the house looking for him. He snuggled on Nils's side of the bed, hung out at the foot of his closet and by his car, and waited for him on the steps of his office. He looked sad; he no longer had his buddy. Oliver was an energetic dog who loved to play and chase balls. He needed that kind of attention and energetic release Nils had given him. Nils would throw him a ball for hours each day, even while he was working. He always gave Oliver partial credit when he came up with a good business strategy. After asking for advice from a few canine professionals, I felt it would be best to find Oliver a great home with a super new parent, lots of room to frolic, and some other dogs to hang out with.

At just the right moment, a friend asked if I would let her adopt Oliver. Tears welled in my eyes. She had six other dogs and acres of land. I met her in Geneva a few days later, holding Oliver tightly to my chest while lavishing him with hugs and kisses. I reminded him how much Nils loved him and how much I loved him, and I gently gave him to my friend and asked her to take incredibly good care of him. She took him for the weekend to see if he would fit in. On Monday she called and said she and the other dogs loved him! A part of me hadn't wanted it to work out. I felt like I was letting Oliver and Nils down. But

I also knew that I wouldn't be able to meet Oliver's needs now that I was alone. I'm grateful I was open to doing the right thing for Oliver, even though it was difficult.

Then, almost a year after Nils's death, I knew the time had arrived for me to leave the house I'd shared with Nils, his children, and the dogs, even though I could still hear echoes of the dogs running about, my step kids' laughter, and all of us sitting on the couch watching movies. I could still see in my mind's eye Emma's and Mia's teenage bedrooms with stuff strewn everywhere and Clara's and Charlie's rooms, where I'd spent so many nights curled up with them reading bedtime stories. I felt tethered to the space that had been filled with so much love and laughter, but I knew that an integral part of letting go was moving from the house.

My friends John and Raushana encouraged me to move in with them. They lived across Lake Geneva in France. I agreed, but then I kept postponing the date. One afternoon, my car was packed, Quantum, our other dog, was in the front seat, and I drove toward the front gate. As the gate opened, I put the car in reverse and went back. I did that half a dozen times before bursting into tears. We took refuge in the carport, and I didn't answer my phone. The following day, a sunny afternoon in April 2012, John came over and helped Quantum and me drive away. I never went back. It was a monumental step.

John and Raushana opened their home with enough love to steady me, and being around their children—Ariana, Brandon, and Shaun—boosted my spirits. Birthdays were celebrated, there were intense discussions about school attendance and study, meals were shared, and laughter and music echoed throughout their home. Moving from Collonge-Bellerive was critical for letting go of attachments and past associations, and to begin to embrace a new life.

But before moving back to the US, I wanted to return Nils's wedding ring to him on Mont Blanc, the one he wore every day of our marriage. Energetically Mont Blanc felt like the perfect place for Nils's ring to be. At the suggestion of a friend, I reached out to an accomplished climber named Freddie, a member of our fellowship who had summited Mont Blanc several times, to ask if he would support my climbing the mountain to do this.

I met Freddie at a meeting and made my request. He asked if I'd ever climbed a mountain, and when I said no, he explained that Mont Blanc is the tallest mountain in the Alps and Western Europe and that even experienced climbers die every year ascending and descending the mountain. He paused and then asked, "Why do you want to climb this mountain?" My response was simple, "I buried my husband there in May. It was Nils's second-favorite place to be on the planet, and I want to leave his wedding band at the summit." I was sure Freddie would understand my spiritual motivation. I also told him that I needed to take on a challenge that would test me physically and mentally—and would distract me from Nils's absence. Amazingly, he agreed and even felt it would benefit him, too, since he'd never taken anyone to the summit before.

I trained by going on six-hour hikes up and down a mountain trail near John and Raushana's house carrying a twenty-pound pack, five days a week. I had focus and determination, and I got stronger and stronger physically, mentally, and emotionally. In celebration of Nils's life—and a fulfillment of my commitment, training, and deep desire to continue on my spiritual journey—I climbed Mont Blanc on June 23, 2012, barely a year after Nils's death. I was successful in getting close to the Refuge Bivouac Vallot which is at 4,362 meters (14,311 feet), the last hut before reaching the Summit at 4,810 meters (15,784 feet). It's used for shelter from unexpected storms, tired climbers, restroom breaks, a change of clothes, necessities at those heights. I knew it was quite an accomplishment for someone who had only gone up to the top of a mountain by a chairlift or telecabine. Freddie did an outstanding job encouraging me and keeping me safe. He was firm and clear with his directions, and asked me to communicate only with him about the task at hand, and to focus on each step I took and each rock I grabbed.

Adrenaline was coursing through me, and chit-chatting seemed to calm my nerves, but it didn't help my focus, so I climbed in silence, concentrating on my breath and spoke only when Freddie asked me a question. We were about to traverse a portion of the mountain called Grand Couloir, known as the Corridor of Death. It can be extremely dangerous due its steepness—the gradient averages 80 percent—falling rocks and ice, and in dry conditions, there may not be enough snow to bind the loose rocks together. There's a cable fixed to the mountain, so climbers can clip on as they pass through. We were roped together, so any misstep by either of us could have harmed us both. Ensuring both our safety meant following his directions to the letter. Mont Blanc is one of the most challenging peaks to climb in Europe—the weather is always changing; the terrain is unpredictable; and the altitude makes it difficult for even experienced climbers to acclimate. I was an inexperienced climber and didn't want to endanger Freddie's life.

We reached Tête Rousse Hut, where we met two Polish climbers, one of whom was as accomplished as Freddie. We ended up pitching a tent on the snow, because neither of us had reservations to stay at the Refuge du Goûter, which turned out to be somewhat problematic. Freddie had waited too late to book, and the Polish men had planned to climb to Goûter in the morning. Making the best of it all, we enjoyed a wonderful meal with a vast view of the Chamonix valley and saw a breathtaking sunset.

We shared the purpose of our climbs, and agreed that if conditions became difficult after Goûter, Freddie and the experienced Polish climber would make the final ascent with Nils's ring. It was exhilarating to sleep under the stars at 3,167 meters (10,390 feet).

We all got up early and began to climb to the Refuge du Goûter at 3,835 meters (12,582 feet), but we would soon learn that we hadn't gotten up early enough. Looking up at the sheer rocky incline was overwhelming—even more shocking than the Grand Couloir because we would have to "scramble," a combination of rock climbing and hiking. I had to take it one intentional step at a time and be careful that what I grabbed was sturdy enough to help move me up the mountain. Some of the rocks were loose, damp, and icy. I thought everyone around me could hear my heart pounding. Climbing with crampons was extremely challenging on the rocky portion up to Goûter, as they're meant to grab

ice and snow. There were climbers ahead of us and behind us. It was —simultaneously—terrifying and exhilarating.

As we reached the refuge, I felt alive. It became clear why Nils loved this mountain so much. *It was simply breathtaking.* Conditions did, in fact, change, so we switched partners as we had agreed. Without hesitation, I reached deep in my pocket and gave Nils's ring to Freddie and asked him to send Nils love and light. To my surprise, Freddie asked if he could wear the ring on the ascent. I was profoundly touched and said, "Absolutely." There was something deeply spiritual about having Freddie—a man who loves life and loves the mountains, who was sober, and who had children of his own—wear Nils's ring for the last leg of the climb up Mont Blanc.

My new Polish partner and I continued to climb until we met some very experienced climbers who had a message from Freddie to start our descent to Goûter and wait for him there. We were tethered to one another, fatigued, and in awe of the slow, methodical walk to the summit on the sparkling white snow, while being extremely mindful of our footing because of possible crevasses (fissures) or falling snow. This

made the climb dangerous, because you never knew where a crevasse might be, so staying on the path was critical. The crampons were easier to navigate on the snow and ice though, and fortunately, I did not have any issues with the altitude.

Ironically, the more I let go of Nils, the more I could feel his presence. Nils had climbed Mont Blanc many times with friends, and I know he was sitting somewhere on the mountain having a good chuckle. I felt his appreciation, love, and gratitude—knowing he was now here, and throughout the world. I'm sure it brought him joy that someone loved him enough to do that—how willing I was to go to the ends of the earth for him.

Freddie made it to the summit and kept his promise to leave Nils's wedding band there. Upon his return, he showed me three beautiful photographs of him tossing Nils's ring. He made it clear that he tossed the ring on the Italian side and he added, "Kimberly, the fact that you were able to let go of something that meant so much to you is testimony to your love for Nils, and now you can live your entire life knowing his ring is where it belongs, with him on his favorite mountain forever." Again, I was touched by Freddie's words and could feel the changes taking place in me. My heart felt more whole.

We spent the night at Goûter hut with a dozen or so other climbers and witnessed another breathtaking sunset. I felt emotionally, mentally, and physically stronger because of the climb, more confident that everything would work itself out and that I would be okay. At around that moment, I realized that we still had to descend the mountain that we'd just climbed.

The descent proved as challenging as the ascent. We left early the next morning because a storm was coming. Again, Freddie asked me to be present, stay focused, and be quiet as we made our way back down the steep terrain and back across the dangerous Grand Couloir. I felt more confidant in my abilities, but my body was full of nervous energy and excitement. Remembering to focus on my breathing really helped me find my center. By Grace, we made it down safely. and I was proud of myself for staying calm and getting both up and down the mountain without any injuries except for a blister on my heel and some extremely fatigued muscles. Once we arrived back at the car and changed into more cozy clothing, including swapping our mountaineering boots for tennis shoes, we decided to have dinner and take in the enormity of what we had accomplished. It was a life affirming experience which forced me to get really uncomfortable. The challenges on the mountain reminded me of the necessity of taking risks which can lead to unexpected opportunities like meeting Freddie. Freddie suggested we go to the village of Chamonix, where we strolled through the cobbled streets, browsing the menus on display, walking through the sport shops, and enjoying the magnificence of Mont Blanc. I could feel Nils's presence everywhere in Chamonix. It was a wonderful way to have closure and an exhilarating and incredible experience!

*   *   *

I had loved living in Switzerland, but because I was feeling unsafe, I knew moving back to the US made sense, even if I was still unsure about it. When I moved from the house in Collonge-Bellerive, all I shipped back to the US were my personal items and a few of Nils's things like his smelly ASICS running shoes. Everything else was still in the house, which was fine with me. I actually felt freer with fewer possessions. Living with John and Raushana was perfect preparation to take my next steps.

More than a year after Nils's death, John took Quantum and me to Geneva Airport. As I checked my bags and headed through security and passport control, once again, a flood of memories and emotions came rushing through my body. I boarded an early-morning flight to New York with my dog and personal belongings. I had scheduled a long layover in New York to spend some time in Central Park, appreciate the condo where Nils and I had lived, and visit the wall in front of the Apple Store, where I knew I was going to marry him. I got to honor these sacred spaces while saying thank you to Nils for all the experiences we'd shared.

It was a beautiful day in New York; Central Park was bustling with people walking, running, and riding bikes. Quantum and I were lying on the grass, and I was appreciating the architecture of the Plaza, and taking in the energy of the park in the very place Nils and I were married and spent so much time in love with the magical feeling of Manhattan. The sun was shining and a gentle breeze caressed my face. I could see our living room and bedroom windows, remembering the many times I sat looking out those windows appreciating the beauty of Central Park, while Nils was at another window taking photos.

I brought one of Nils's favorite hoodies to give to someone in need in Central Park. Nils used to buy dozens of donuts for the homeless in the park, and I wanted to do something to honor that practice of his. For a brief moment as I handed a homeless man the hoodie, I had a glimpse of Nils's spirit in the stranger's eyes. Something mystical happened. I saw love in this man's eyes and was able to let go a little bit more. I left the park feeling at peace and grateful for all the days, hours, and minutes Nils and I had spent together. After three hours in Central Park that day, Quantum and I went by taxi to JFK Airport to fly to Los Angeles.

Within days of moving back to the United States, I started to feel unrooted. Wanting community, I attended a Mass at St. Monica, my childhood church. I needed to be around people and places that were familiar and filled with spirit. The church's interior is breathtaking, ornate with super-high ceilings while faith, forgiveness, love, and courage fill the space even when no one is there. There was an announcement at the end of a church service that a grief support group would be starting the following week, and I hesitantly joined. The group lasted for three months. There were twenty of us, and everyone seemed to have a different need. Some were addressing issues related to a loved one who had died years earlier; a few were there because a loved one had just died recently, and they were attempting to hold on and sort things out; and others felt stuck in their grieving process and hoped the group might help.

At the conclusion of the grief support group, each of us was invited to submit a photo of our loved one, to be displayed on a large screen during the church's Mass of Remembrance. I submitted a beautiful yet playful photograph of Nils wearing his ski suspenders, ski pants rolled up to his knees, with a gigantic smile on his face. Patrick, who had been the witness at our wedding in New York, happened to be in Los Angeles on business the weekend of the Mass, and he stood by my side to honor his friend's passing. When Nils's picture came on the screen, my parents, Patrick, and I all cried and held one another. Day by day, in honoring and remembering, I was able to feel my love and gratitude for Nils more deeply, and in the process, I was able to let go a little bit more.

These grief support group sessions helped me make the highly emotional decision to stop wearing my engagement and wedding rings. I loved wearing these rings and deeply felt the symbolism behind them. They were by now a part of me. Nils had bought my engagement ring in Geneva and surprised me with it when he proposed in New York. We picked out my wedding ring on a beautiful weekday afternoon on Fifth Avenue. The saleswoman asked us each to select a ring and place it on the counter without the other person being in the room. We both picked the same style, but Nils chose one with larger diamonds. She was surprised that I had selected the one with the smaller diamonds. It was one of the few times Nils and I shopped together, and it was a sweet experience.

Letting go of my rings meant no longer wearing them. I wrestled with this for more than a year, speaking to several widows. I'd take them off, and my finger felt naked without them, so I put them back on. Not wearing them felt dishonoring our life together. I became hyper focused on people's ring fingers. *Is he married, is she engaged, are they happy, is he sober, do they live honestly, will they be together forever?* I remember looking at the rings on my finger one afternoon with so much love and a sense that they represented Nils and that wearing them was one small way of staying physically connected with him. But I also felt like they had become my own scarlet letter because of the guilt that continued to surface from time to time for having been unable to save him. I did finally take them off and put them in a satin satchel. I still look at them and hold them occasionally, for they are symbols of the impermanence and the exquisiteness of life.

In addition to the grief support group, I began attending a 7:30 a.m. 12-step meeting that included ten minutes of meditation at a center called Against the Stream. Sitting quietly with others whether on a cushion or in a chair each morning helped me feel more secure and connected and reduced my anxiety. Meditation centers provide a place to sit with others and to explore teachings that encourage awareness in daily life. Slowly but surely, I was letting go of the irretrievable past and stepping into the present, and my life began to open in new and surprising ways.

This is where I met Craig, a spiritual, sober soul. He entered the meditation room as I was standing at the doorway greeting people. As he approached, he felt very familiar to me. Just as I'd known while sitting outside the Apple Store in New York all those years earlier that Nils and I would be together, I had a strong premonition that Craig was going to be in my life in a powerful way.

A month or so later, Craig invited me to join him visiting a couple of spiritual sites in the LA area. I'm a curious person and had no idea what the day would include but was eager to join him. The first stop was the Self-Realization Fellowship's Lake Shrine Temple in the Pacific Palisades, a world-renowned oasis of peace and meditation. We walked around the luscious grounds, visited the church, and spent some time in the meditation room before browsing through the gift shop and buying some incense. Next, we went to the Malibu Hindu Temple in the hills of Calabasas. We arrived in time to participate in the *puja* (worship)—where bells were ringing, incense permeated the air, flowers and fruits were offered, and prayers recited. We got to participate in the *arti*, a ceremony of light conducted at the end of the puja in which a flame is waved to remove the darkness. The depth of faith in the room was palpable. Here was a large group of people who felt like a real family expressing thanksgiving. As the arti flame passed them, each person cupped their downturned hands over the flame and then raised their palms to their faces to receive the blessings. After the ceremony, we spent time in the large courtyard that had marble statues of Hindu deities, supernatural beings considered to be divine or sacred, in each corner.

Craig introduced me to these gods and goddesses—Rama, Lakshmana, Sita, Hanuman, Maha Lakshmi, Krishna, and Radha. In the lower temple, he introduced me to Ganesha, Shiva, Parvati, Vishnu, and others. Before leaving we were given *prasad* (specially prepared vegetarian food) to eat, a gracious gift that had been blessed by the temple priest. Everything felt familiar, as though I'd been there before, and I knew I'd be back.

God's hands were mysteriously guiding us that day, and our final stop was the noon arti at the LA Hare Krishna Center. As Craig was driving us there, my mind was thinking about the Krishnas I'd seen at airports, men wrapped in orange cloth with shaved heads (except for small ponytails) jumping up and down and singing. Still, my heart was open as we entered the temple and saw one of the devotees opening the wooden panels to reveal the exquisitely dressed images of Krishna and Radha. At that moment, other devotees began to play lovely music and sing the Govindam song, then the Hare Krishna chant. It was so beautiful I fell to my knees, tears streaming down my cheeks. *I was home.* The Hare Krishna chant resonated deep within me, and I was drawn to Krishna, who is revered as the god of compassion, protection, tenderness, and love. It was as though Krishna knew everything about my journey and held me in his loving gaze. After my experiences seeing the Krishna people in airports, it was a wonderful and pleasant surprise to have these feelings override the judgments I'd harbored. Today I see only the beauty of their devotion.

As the arti came to a close, my heart felt lighter, quieter, happier, and more resolved. I knew I'd had a life-changing spiritual experience. Krishna reassured me that Nils, the kids, and I were all okay, and that there was nothing to fear and nothing to hold on to from my past. He whispered ever so softly that my love for them dwells deep within my soul and can never be taken from me, and he advised me to cherish and embrace this love, and that will keep us connected forever. I left some pieces of my past at the Krishna Temple that day. The energy and devotion in this sacred space provided an unexpected opening, allowing me to let go even further.

The next day, I went to the gift shop at the Krishna Center and bought two necklaces, which I've worn every day since. One is a long strand of small tulsi beads that wraps around my neck three times, and the other a strand of small tulsi beads with a Narasimha pendant. I was unconsciously drawn to Narasimha and found out later that he is the Great Protector and that tulsi beads have healing properties. While I was at the shop, Craig called to see how I was doing and what I was doing. I shyly told him I was back at the Krishna Center. He laughed and was clearly touched that the activities from the day before had affected me deeply.

Craig and Cynthia, who is my current sponsor, were instrumental in my going to India. They both felt being there would help me continue to release unresolved emotions and bring me clarity. Cynthia suggested that I bring something that had belonged to Nils that I would be willing to let go of. In the last moments in the intensive care unit, I had cut off a large lock of his hair and had been planning to keep it in a secure place for the rest of my life. With Cynthia's prompt, I decided to take it with me to India. She was confident that India, with all its contradictions, would help me in ways I might not understand, and would help Nils too. She was right on both counts. Going to India saved, and changed, my life. Most sponsors, I believe, not being familiar with India and its spiritual practices, would probably have advised me not to go, that it was too soon and would disrupt my routine, as I had been back in the US for just six months. I'll always be grateful to Craig and Cynthia for knowing before I did how important this trip would be.

After our wonderful experiences in Varanasi, Adrianne, Huner, Craig, and I took a flight to New Delhi, where we were greeted by a driver named Sandeep and driven to Rishikesh. Along the way, we stopped at Neem Karoli Baba's ashram to pay our respects. My introduction to Neem Karoli Baba (also known as Maharaj-ji, or Baba) took place in Craig's car the day he showed me around LA. Craig has a small picture of Baba and Swamiji on his dashboard. Neem Karoli Baba was a Hindu guru, devotee of Hanuman, and known in the West as the guru of Ram Dass, and also of Krishna Das, Shyam Das, Bhagavan Das, and other American teachers.

When we arrived at the ashram, the sun had just set and it was drizzling. We took off our shoes as we entered and could hear people chanting. Maharaj-ji passed away in 1973, and we walked toward a stunning marble statue of him, and as is custom, got on our knees and prayed. I could feel Maharaj-ji smiling at me and thanking me for finally coming home. This was an auspicious experience for me, and I got goose bumps, so happy to be in his presence. Tears of joy welled up in my eyes. I asked him to keep Nils safe and help him find his way. The small group of us remained sitting for nearly thirty minutes, then off we went. I could have spent the night at his feet. A calmness and courage came over me, and I was struck by the knowledge that everything was perfect in an imperfect way.

It took us a full day to arrive in Rishikesh, exhausted and happy. We checked in at the Divine Resort, a small hotel built on the side of a mountain overlooking the River Ganga. The following day we walked across a footbridge through a small village and up a steep hill filled with tall green banyan and peepal trees to an ashram. Upon arrival, we were escorted to a small outdoor area, where I was introduced to Swami

Prem Varni, our traveling companions' friend who has lived in the area most of his life.

Prem Varni is a spiritual teacher who studied with Maharishi Mahesh Yogi and Sri Tat Wale Baba. His Sri Swami Balyogi Premvarni Ashram is in the Himalayas overlooking the Ganges. After we'd spent several hours with him, I asked for his help. I told him I had a lock of my late husband's hair and wanted to let it go in the river. He hugged me and wiped the tears from my cheeks and said, "Okay."

The next day we all piled in our minivan and traveled to a remote area of the Ganges. The river was flowing gently but powerfully, the mountains were singing, and there was a lovely breeze. Swami Prem Varni grabbed my hand and held the lock of Nils's hair for several minutes while praying in Sanskrit. Then he gave it back to me with a handful of flower petals and encouraged me to let him go and give him to Mother Ganga. Tears were streaming down my face as I gently and lovingly tossed Nils's hair and the petals into the Ganga. I felt Nils holding me and whispering, "Thank you for loving me enough to leave my body on the Mont Blanc, my wedding band at the top of the Mont Blanc, and my hair in one of the most spiritual places on earth." It was a moment I'll always remember. A few minutes later, Craig and I waded into the frigid river water and dunked ourselves three times. There is a belief that healing will come to anyone who does that. When we reached shore, I felt invigorated and lighter.

The following day we made our way from Rishikesh to Allahabad, the site of the Maha Kumbh Mela, a festival held every twelve years, the date determined by Vedic astrology. It involves ritual bathing at Triveni Sangam, the confluence of three holy rivers: the Ganga, the Yamuna, and the invisible Sarasvati. It is the largest spiritual gathering in the world, with over 120 million visitors, mostly Hindus, many traveling hundreds of miles to attend. There were thousands of colorful camps, millions of people milling about, live chanting, food and chai stands, and the fragrant smell of incense permeating the air.

We had the good fortune of staying at the H. H. Pujya Swami Chidanand Saraswatiji (Muniji) Parmarth Niketan camp in the heart of the

Kumbh. From there, we took a very long walk to Swamiji's camp to pay our respects to him and his devotees. Adrianne was committed to finding it among the hundreds of camps, multiple bridges, and thousands of people we had to navigate through. After a few hours of walking, we reached it and were able to say hello to him and the other swamis before they went for a swim.

I wanted to join, but it wasn't possible because I'm a woman. Before Craig left to bathe, he introduced me to Swami Vishwa Paranthapanada, visiting from South Africa. He has a robust personality and stands out in a crowd with his dreadlocks and tattoos. He and I had an epic conversation about life. Even though we'd just met, we are old souls. We sliced through the drama and ended up in the reservoir of the heart which is beyond words. He has become a dear friend and confidant. We talk about life stuff often, always with some humor. I also discovered that one can let go through laughter. I fondly call him Swami P.

After a few hours at camp, we headed off to the holy river to bathe. Craig and I passed a man with no arms and no legs crawling to the Ganga. We both felt this man might have been a holy man or a saint. He was clearly determined to get to the river on his own. We were speechless. Many asked if they could help, but he declined. His courage and faith touched my heart deeply. How can one complain about the inconveniences of life after witnessing this? An experience like this helps put life into perspective. Craig and I were blessed to bathe on one of the main bathing dates. Adrianne opted not to but watched us. Thousands of men, women, and children were bathing as we entered the water—smiling, laughing, praying, hugging one another, some tossing flowers into the water, others submerging themselves three times while praying, a magnificent display of faith.

Craig and I submerged ourselves three times while expressing our wishes and offering our prayers. The possibility came to me that Nils and I would both be free. Once we were back on the bank of the river, Adrianne handed Craig and me towels and my small pocketbook. I reached inside for the wallet-sized photo of Nils, the kids, and me that

I'd been carrying since it was taken years earlier at the American Museum of Natural History in New York. It was dear and sacred to me; I valued it more than anything, and I realized my attachment to it—and the longing for the children was only adding to my grief. I held it close to my heart before laying it in the sacred water. Craig and I asked the gods to take care of them as the beautiful family photo merged with the floating flowers and became one with the river.

To let go of something means to release its grip. I'm trusting something profound will happen for all because of this spontaneous act. Letting go happens a million different ways over days, months, and years, not just physically, but in all the ways we've grown accustomed to a person. For me, that meant letting go of being able to physically hold him, to talk to him about his day, to wake up next to him snoring, to kiss his forehead, his cheeks, and his lips before he went to work, and to watch us grow old together. It meant letting go of the life we'd created in Switzerland with volunteer organizations, close friends, and my step kids. It was *extremely* challenging, but letting go of what was familiar was the only way to open the door to new possibilities.

Letting go of that photo in that moment involved trusting in the gods that there was more for me to do somewhere else. As Ram Dass beautifully explains, our ego has a difficult time with letting go of the physical form, but our love transcends any change, including death. The love we feel keeps us connected to our loved ones who have passed away. Letting go of significant aspects of the past has allowed me to experience the fullness of my new life and the enormous love I still feel for Nils and the life we had in Switzerland. I will always treasure the memories I have.

We hold on to each other, our memories of love, the beauty of recognizing each other in ourselves and the communion of souls, and all the new and surprising Grace-filled experiences that continue to fill our lives. We get to choose to let go of our attachment to outcomes and things we no longer need. What causes suffering is not the memories, not Nils's favorite worn-out sneakers, but our desperate desire to go back to that time or to change what happened. Through letting go, we get to welcome inevitable change, cherish our memories, and appreciate the value of a few personal items we choose to hold on to as keepsakes.

The watch Nils was wearing when I found him in the carport is on the arm of Krishna in Craig's prayer room and will always be precious to me. Seeing it with Krishna and holding it myself from time to time helps me acknowledge the past, the present, and all they entail. When we embrace life as it is and accept what we cannot change, we become empowered. By facing pain and even thanking it, we can grow, and live, and love again.

I have personally experienced the power of surrender—letting go of those I love, and also letting go of beliefs, ways of being, and the things that no longer serve me. Grieving, healing, and letting go take time and require presence and action. They demand that we hold death in our hands, climb proverbial (or real) mountains, immerse ourselves in the healing waters of life, and do whatever it takes to move through the darkness into the light. There are some memories embedded in my being, like the votive candles that illuminated the darkness and deepened our prayers in Varanasi, the flowers floating down the sacred Ganga in Rishikesh carrying Nils's lock of hair away from me, and Freddie putting on Nils's wedding ring just before ascending to the summit of Mont Blanc. I unwittingly accepted and received a new life each time I gave Nils back to Mother Earth.

It is in giving that we receive. Each moment I let go of a physical part of Nils, I feel an overwhelmingly beautiful divine energy—Grace. It is there all the time, of course, but when I am awake and present, surrendering to what is, I can feel it. *What is,* is to be embraced. *What is,* is to be celebrated. *What is,* is the reality that Nils remains with me forever. When I let go of the *idea* of what my life should be, I am able to surrender to the new life that awaits me, life unfolding in all its beautiful textures and colors while I am in the "queue."

CHAPTER 9

Dancing with the Divine

Abide in the heart and surrender your acts to the Divine.
— RAMANA MAHARSHI

Nils's death increased my grit and resolve to stay sober—as well as conscious, respectful, and thankful—and I have resisted all labeling of my grieving as pathology, because I've known in my soul, even in the darkest moments, that each experience and stage of grief, even those that were extreme, were in some way "normal." When a mental health diagnosis is helpful for self-understanding and obtaining needed help, I'm all for it. In my case, I have felt that Spirit is guiding me, offering great resources like my sponsors, the 12-step program, and spontaneous signposts and gifts.

Mindfulness is the practice of being fully aware of the present moment, free of filters. It takes practice to observe your thoughts and emotions, whether about the past, future, or present, without reacting to them. When you think of this kind of effort, you may envision a Zen monk meditating in the lotus position, but it can be practiced throughout the day—in words, actions, interactions, and even inaction. Nils and I incorporated mindfulness practices into our life at home with the children.

When I became a part of the family, a lovely nanny was helping Nils with the children—driving them to school, helping them with homework, cooking their meals, and tending to their overall well-being. I was excited and honored to be folded into his family, and was willing and wanting to help in any way I could. I insisted that we do all those activities together and that Nils and I play a more integral role in raising his children, so we let the nanny go. This was new to Nils, but he caught on quickly and became intensely interested in his children's daily activities. Nils never did anything halfway; even spending time with his kids, he was all in.

Nils wanted the kids to excel in school, so doing homework with them was important to him. An intense, passionate man, Nils was enthusiastic about many things, some of which the kids weren't, and his enthusiasm was sometimes overbearing and created strong reactions. He didn't yell, but he changed his usually friendly, warm tone to a stronger and firmer one when he wanted to be taken seriously. I felt it was important for his kids to feel empowered and supported, to know that their feelings mattered, so I suggested that they select an "interrupt word" when they felt he wasn't listening or was getting too intense. The kids chose *teapot*.

Having four kids speaking three languages, all talking over each other, Nils would at times raise his voice to get their attention. They would all stop, and together respond, "Teapot, Papa!" He usually laughed, and it made us all more aware of our interactions. When Nils lost his cool while helping them with homework, the kids would say, "Teapot, Papa," reminding him to chill. The phrase would stop him in his tracks and empower the kids. Sometimes it was necessary, and at other times, it was a way to ease tension and add a splash of humor.

As I was settling into my life without Nils as my protector, I had to draw on all the spiritual, clinical, and self-help tools I'd learned from years of reading books, listening to tapes, attending sessions with wisdom keepers, going to meetings, and meditating to remain conscious in my interactions. Each time I attend a meeting, I rededicate myself to sobriety and to a spiritual way of life. It's a room full of souls caring about one another is uplifting and energizing. Mindful awareness helps us to take responsibility for one's perceptions and communications, verbal and nonverbal.

There were times I wanted to push back against the egregious behavior of some individuals, but I knew deep inside I would not be able to influence their actions. So, I simply witnessed without exploding. I called on my own version of *teapot,* especially in those early years. Lashing out might have brought some temporary relief, but I had the presence of mind—despite feeling at times like I was on the verge of flying off the handle—to know that I am responsible for my actions and that if I acted on these impulses, I would, at the very least, have to make amends later.

I survived those first few years after Nils's death because of my deep commitment to staying sober, which included going to meetings, working the 12 steps, staying close to my supportive and sober friends, and continuing to learn from self-help teachings, including the ones I had thrown in the trash. No one can survive life's traumas alone. We need love, support and companionship, and we deserve the space to do our healing. Meetings offered a place to be real, to practice compassion, and to share my gratitude. It was such a beautiful experience to center my day in a place of spirit, where I was encouraged and supported, and where I could support and give back to others as well.

It can be challenging to stay present and have compassion for those we feel have harmed us. But the way through is to be honest and remain aware of our true nature, which is love. I pray daily that everyone is surrounded by love, and before I know it, I too feel more love. The meetings I attend regularly start with reading aloud a portion of Chapter 5, "How It Works," from *The Big Book.* I listen intently as though I'm hearing it for the first time:

> *Rarely have we seen a person fail who has thoroughly followed our path. Those who do not recover are people who cannot or will not completely give themselves to this simple program, usually men and women who are constitutionally incapable of being honest with themselves. There are such unfortunates. They are not at fault; they seem to have been born that way. They are naturally incapable of grasping and developing a manner of living which demands rigorous honesty. Their chances are less than average. There are those, too, who suffer from grave emotional and mental*

disorders, but many of them do recover if they have the capacity to be honest.

Our stories disclose in a general way what we used to be like, what happened, and what we are like now. If you have decided that you want what we have and are willing to go to any length to get it - then you are ready to take certain steps.

At some of these we balked. We thought we could find an easier, softer way. But we could not. With all the earnestness at our command, we beg of you to be fearless and thorough from the very start. Some of us have tried to hold on to our old ideas and the result was nil until we let go absolutely.

Remember that we deal with addiction—cunning, baffling, powerful! Without help it is too much for us. But there is One who has all power—that One is God. May you find him now.

When I hear these words, tears well up in my eyes and I think of Nils, who was unable to acknowledge the seriousness of his addiction and his need for help. The program didn't fail Nils; it's that Nils didn't make sobriety and being an active member of a 12-step program a priority. If he had, they would have been the most important commitments of his life. It's essential to admit complete defeat and become willing to go to any lengths to get sober and stay sober. He was unable to ask for help and admit complete defeat. It's possible he was constitutionally incapable of being honest with himself with regard to his addiction. He had experienced trauma, like many of us. He shared so many sorrows, regrets, joys, and passions with me, but there were things he felt he couldn't share with anyone.

This is the beauty of being involved with a spiritual community—we find that we aren't alone, that there's a place we can share what's going on, dance with the divine, and know there is a way through: a solution. Nils shouldered a tremendous amount of responsibility, personally and professionally. He thought turning his life over to a higher power was a sign of weakness. The irony is that being vulnerable, asking for help and guidance, is a sign of strength. I, too, thought he would muddle through and get sober again. But Nils was conned by his addictions, believing he was in control and that his life and those he loved were not in danger, even while he continued using periodically.

My friend Sri M told me that suicide is a person's attempt to escape pain. Wanting to be free from suffering is understandable, yet many people want to cast out those who suffer from addictions or mental health issues and those who feel so desperate to be free from pain that they take their own lives. People judge them for not having enough willpower or believe that it's a choice not to get help. Imagine the loneliness and desperation a person must experience in the moments preceding their death, feeling no one can help them. They've lost all hope and may feel unworthy, believing they are beyond salvation, that there's nothing left for them. Some may feel embarrassed or disgraced for their addictions, their mental health issues, or the pain they've caused others. When we look at life from this point of view, we may feel more love and vulnerability.

It's okay to be feel lost. It's okay to feel obliterated. It's okay to feel uncertain. It's okay to question everything. Expressing ourselves is healthy; there's no need for self-flagellation. Ram Dass wrote a letter to a couple whose child, Rachel, was murdered. Though he writes specifically to Rachel's parents, it's a letter to all of us.

> *Dear Steve and Anita,*
>
> *Rachel finished her work on earth and left the stage in a manner that leaves those of us left behind with a cry of agony in our hearts, as the fragile thread of our faith is dealt with so violently. Is anyone strong enough to stay conscious through such teaching as you are receiving? Probably very few. And even they would only have a whisper of equanimity and peace amidst the screaming trumpets of their rage, grief, horror, and desolation.*
>
> *I can't assuage your pain with any words, nor should I. For your pain is Rachel's legacy to you. Not that she or I would inflict such pain by choice, but there it is. And it must burn its purifying way to completion. For something in you dies when you bear the*

unbearable, and it is only in that dark night of the soul that you
are prepared to see as God sees, and to love as God loves.

Now is the time to let your grief find expression. No false
strength. Now is the time to sit quietly and speak to Rachel and
thank her for being with you these few years and encourage her to
go on with whatever her work is, knowing that you will grow in
compassion and wisdom from this experience. In my heart, I know
that you will meet again, and recognize the many ways in which
you have known each other. And when you meet you will know, in
a flash, what now it is not given to you to know: Why this had to
be the way it was.

Our rational minds can never understand what has hap-
pened, but our hearts—if we can keep them open to God—will
find their own intuitive way. Rachel came through you to do her
work on earth, which includes her manner of death. Now her soul
is free, and the love that you can share with her is invulnerable to
the winds of changing time and space.

In that deep love, include me.
Ram Dass

Reading Ram Dass's letter was incredibly helpful, put a lot into perspective, and changed me. He begins by beautifully and eloquently
expressing what it's like to lose someone to violence "amidst the screaming trumpets of . . . rage, grief, horror, and desolation." He doesn't try to
assuage the parents' pain or grief but advises them to let it "burn its
purifying way to completion." He also advises them to let their "grief
find expression." He warns against false strength and instead says to
show gratitude—thanking Rachel for the years she shared with them
and encouraging her soul to move on, "knowing that you will grow in
compassion and wisdom" from the experience. He invites her parents
to be conscious, mindful, and nonjudgmental—mainly of themselves—
and asks them to be compassionate and tender with themselves during
this difficult time.

He doesn't offer platitudes. He doesn't judge them for being angry,
sad, or in despair. He kindly, gently, and compassionately says that it's

okay that you're grieving; it's okay that you're sad. You loved your child, and you miss her. He walks them through the grief process gently and reminds them that it's normal. And he does it with gratitude, compassion, and mindfulness, free of judgment: *Our rational minds can never understand what has happened, but our hearts—if we can keep them open to God—will find their own intuitive way. Rachel came through you to do her work on earth, which includes her manner of death. Now her soul is free and the love that you can share with her is invulnerable to the winds of changing time and space.*

I had to find my own "intuitive way" to make peace with Nils's death. He came here and completed his work on earth, *which included the manner of his death*. His soul was now free, and the love that we shared was "invulnerable to the winds of changing time and space." When all else passes away—the love remains. I was encouraged from both Nils's life and his death to keep my heart open. I was encouraged to be vulnerable, open to all—even the pain and the grief—until it burned its way to "purifying completion." I knew that judging myself and others would be counterproductive, but being still in the moment, aware of the emotions I was experiencing, and treating myself and others with empathy and understanding, would serve me (and others) best. I still read Ram Dass's letter to Rachel's parents as a reminder that my love for Nils, and all love, transcends death.

My friend Jack Casey gave me this prayer by Sri Ramana Maharshi, a great Hindu saint, that I find extremely helpful:

Place your burden at the feet of the Lord of the universe who is ever victorious and accomplishes everything. Remain all the time steadfast in the heart, in the Transcendental Absolute. God knows the past, present and future. He will determine the future for you and accomplish the work. What is to be done will be done at the proper time. Don't worry. Abide in the heart and surrender your acts to the Divine.

This is a powerful reminder to trust in a power greater than you. *What is to be done will be done at the proper time. Don't worry. Abide in the heart and surrender.* To me, this says it all. It's such a comfort and a relief to know that everything—our sorrow, our worries, our stress, and our brokenness—can be placed at the feet of the Lord of the Universe. It doesn't mean we sit around and do nothing. We do what we can, knowing that the rest is being taken care of. This simple yet not-so-simple act of surrendering, of letting my higher power take perfect care of me and everyone, is what I strive for every day. I posted this prayer on my office wall and on my refrigerator, and I read it every morning.

We will never know all the whys in life. We will never be able to control or predict the future. And we certainly can't change or undo the past. All we have is *now*, the eternal now. The rest is a mystery and wonder. We can embrace one moment at a time with grace and gratitude, and when we do, the suffering becomes manageable and, eventually, things get brighter. We can choose to live mindfully and to dance with divine. Any dance will do, it's up to your imagination. As Ram Dass wrote to Rachel's parents, the *Big Book* conveys, and Sri Ramana Maharshi writes: "Abide in your heart, and surrender your acts to the Divine." We are exactly where we need to be, and as Debbie so wisely observed, *"Everything is falling together."*

CHAPTER 10

Reconnecting with Love

*Your task is not to seek for love, but merely to seek and find all the barriers
within yourself that you have built against it.*
— RUMI

A lthough I often describe my life with Nils as a fairy tale, we met
under stressful circumstances in a rehab facility. On July 3, 2007,
I entered treatment after a relapse with alcohol. It was one of the lowest
points in my life. I'd been sober for fourteen years from a cocaine and
prescription pill addiction and had built up a reputation in the recovery world. At one point, I was even running a prominent treatment
center in California.

My relapse was a shock to me. I loved being sober and helping others get sober, but somewhere along the way I neglected my own program, which led to my relapse. I began to be more concerned about
what others thought of me than about my own health and wellness. To
admit that I needed to go back to treatment was challenging. I felt so
ashamed, I struggled with walking into a meeting locally and raising
my hand as a newcomer.

My mom was instrumental in getting me to go. She learned about
Eric Clapton's rehab facility on the Caribbean island of Antigua and
made arrangements for me to go. I agreed, provided I could use an
alias, and I entered treatment as Isabella. Going to treatment in a different country under another name seemed to make sense. All of it seems
improbable and miraculous in hindsight. Today it makes me laugh,

because in rehab I met an incredible man who was full of life and who lived on another continent.

The morning after my arrival, Nils walked up to me and asked why I was so sad. I remember saying to myself, "Why do you think I'm so sad?" I had just admitted myself for treatment in a country far from home. And our friendship began at that moment. We spent a lot of time together talking about his family and life in general. We got up almost every morning at 5:30 to go running together, which was a real treat because he was very competitive and none of the other clients were really interested in exercise. Nils told me he was at the facility to work through some family issues and that he was getting a divorce. But when he spoke about his kids, his eyes started to dance. He was really proud of them and obviously loved them very much. He had a large photo of them on his tablet. I only found out years later that he was in treatment because of a drug and alcohol addiction.

I felt we were old souls who happened to reconnect in Antigua, stimulated by each other's life experiences, views of the world, and the directions we were heading. It was as though we'd known each other for a lifetime. We were not romantically involved, and in fact that never crossed my mind. I was drawn to his energy, intellect, charm, and our mutual desire to get physically fit while at the facility. When Nils walked in the room, he had such a radiant smile and strong presence, people naturally wanted to be near him.

We developed close relationships with two others in Antigua, both of whom I'm still in touch with. Patrick was a witness at our wedding, and Nick is now married with children. Both continue to love being sober. We enjoy staying in touch and celebrating the wonders of life. Other beautiful relationships blossomed from my having the courage—or should I say desperation?—to enter rehab. I am forever grateful to my mom for intervening and insisting that I go.

After we completed our respective treatment programs, Nils and I stayed in touch by phone, and a few months later agreed to meet at a coffee shop in Manhattan. Nils was fashionably late. He called at 10:45 a.m. and told me he was outside. I exited the coffee shop and realized he was at the other end of the block. I started hollering his name, waving my arms, and instinctively began running toward him. He then started running toward me, and I jumped into his arms. We gave each other a big bear hug, and both of us started to cry. He wiped the tears from his eyes and said he was surprised by his strong emotions. I was equally surprised by this overwhelming sense of knowing and loving him deeply. We spent the next four hours sitting on the stone wall outside the Apple Store on Fifth Avenue at 59th Street. We hardly spoke. He had canceled an important appointment so we could just sit there and be silent. It was as though time had stopped. Then we both had to leave to catch a flight home. Nils grabbed me by my arms, kissed me on my lips, and said, "I believe I'm going to marry you." I had the same knowing.

A month later Nils flew to California to meet my family. I went to pick him up at Atlantic Aviation, a short distance from Los Angeles International Airport. His plane was delayed thirty minutes, which seemed like an eternity. I had spent hours deciding what to wear and ended up with a simple loose-fitting dress and a pair of sneakers. I wanted to look beautiful for him. I paced back and forth. When he finally arrived and got off the plane, he dropped his briefcase, and I dropped my purse. We ran to each other and embraced. The pilot and copilot were just standing there waiting for an appropriate moment: "Mr. Nilsson, don't forget your ice cream." Nils blushed and looked at me and said, "I brought you several quarts of amazing ice cream." He had just flown twelve hours and brought me ice cream from Sweden! It doesn't get any sweeter than that.

My family loved him. They found him sweet, generous, interesting, intelligent, and kind, and they loved how happy I looked when I was in his company. My dad in particular really enjoyed getting to know Nils. They had mutual respect from the get-go and had a lot in common with risk taking and real estate.

The day before he left, Nils and I had breakfast at a small café in Manhattan Beach. He looked at me and said we were going to spend the rest of our lives together, and the next day, I flew with him to Sweden to meet his family. I knew it would all sort itself out.

Although it's recommended that those in recovery wait at least a year after becoming sober before dating, Nils and I felt it was the natural thing for us to do. I had a lengthy conversation with my sponsor, and she was supportive because of my previous fourteen years of sobriety. She also made it clear that sobriety had to be my priority if this was going to work. A month later, I was living in New York to begin creating a home for us, and a month after that I was in Switzerland doing the same. My sponsor encouraged me to get connected in the fellowship in both places right away, because both were new to me and very different cultures. Nils felt my enthusiasm for sobriety, and I felt that being active in the program would inspire him to get more involved. He said he was given a new lease on life.

In my early thirties, I developed a passion for handbags, and as part of our new life, I moved my sizable collection. When they arrived in New York, Nils was a bit surprised, and I wasn't sure how we were going to get half of them to Switzerland. But Nils being Nils made it easy. They flew privately with us. As we walked past customs with a trolley full of handbags in Geneva, rather than charging us duty fees, the officer, amused by how many bags I had, just smiled.

When we finally married, I had been sober for seventeen months. We were in love and excited to start the next phase of our life together. Most fairy tales end with a wedding, and ours did, too, though rather than castles and ball gowns it was Central Park and blue jeans. I wanted to get married by the wall in front of the Apple Store, where we'd sat in profound silence, but Nils wanted something more romantic (and with less traffic); so we agreed on Central Park, which was just across the street. We selected the Ladies Pavilion, a historic landmark with a covered gazebo, decorative blue cast iron, and a lovely view of the lake, and were married there on March 9, 2009. Patrick and my mom were our witnesses. It was overcast and drizzling lightly (Nils's sister and his mom were happy to hear this; they believed the rain was good luck) with an occasional glimpse of the sparkling sun—another auspicious sign.

It was a simple affair. We hadn't discussed what we would wear, and when we came out of our rooms at the condominium, we were both wearing jeans. We laughed, knowing we were perfect for each other. Nils wore one of his favorite corduroy sport jackets, a white shirt, black socks, and the black leather Cole Haan tennis shoes he loved. I wore a lacy gray camisole, a paisley print long jacket with various shades of blue (Nils's favorite color), and my favorite cowboy boots. The ceremony was majestic. I circled Nils seven times as an expression of devotion and to symbolize the seven days of creation. Nils was grinning from ear to ear as I did. He stepped on a light bulb wrapped in a cloth, symbolizing that something shattered can never return to its former form, representing our desire never to return to the time before we shared our lives. These were affirmations of my faith in God, Nils's faith in science, and our faith in each other and a declaration that our lives together would be longer than it would take to fit the broken pieces back together.

We wrote our own vows, which were simple and to the point. I promised to love him unconditionally, to be the very best stepmom I could be to his kids, and to wear his black socks whenever I wanted. This made him laugh because he didn't like me wearing his black travel socks. And he asked me to commit to reading the first page of the *Wall Street Journal* every day and watch Al Jazeera News at least twice a week. And, unaware of how our marriage would end, he promised to love me and take care of me until we breathed our last breaths together. Within fifteen minutes, we were pronounced man and wife. I was Mrs. Nils Nilsson. I will always cherish that moment, filled with love, laughter, tears, and gratitude. I felt like Cinderella in blue jeans and cowboy boots, honored to be Mrs. Nils Nilsson. I was proud of my husband, wildly in love with him, and excited about the life we were creating together. Patrick, my mom, Nils, and I took a few fun photos and then walked back to the Plaza Hotel coffee shop for some great dessert.

My mom leaned over and gave us both a big hug with tears streaming down her cheeks. She said to Nils, "I no longer have to worry about Kimberly. I know you will take great care of her." Nils's eyes filled with tears as he squeezed my hand. Afterward, Nils and I walked Patrick and my mom to their taxis and headed upstairs, only to discover that in our excitement to get married, we'd locked our keys in the apartment. We asked the doorman to call a locksmith, and it took a couple of hours for the door to be unlocked. So, Nils and I took a beautiful walk through Central Park, and we passed a watch shop on the way home. Nils suggested buying matching watches to memorialize this big day. This made me laugh because he had a love of faux luxury watches, which he'd discovered in New York, and had developed quite the collection. He bought a sporty watch and put it on immediately. I politely declined; I already owned two beautiful watches and seldom wore either. As we walked out of the shop, his parents and sister phoned to congratulate us.

The next day, we flew to Sweden to spend time with his family and celebrate our marriage. I had a strong knowing that I was exactly where I was supposed to be. I felt safe in Nils's arms, as he did in mine. We loved each other deeply. There was no way in those moments that I could have foreseen that this fairy tale would end in a carport in Collonge-Bellerive just outside Geneva just two years later. Nor could I have foreseen that it would take millennia to put the shattered pieces together again.

After Nils died, I was shattered, and I decided to protect my heart by remaining single. I didn't want to risk loving someone so deeply who could simply vanish as Nils had. I decided to become a nun in a faraway monastery where birds deliver the mail. The priest in Switzerland told me I was too old to become a Catholic nun, while my Buddhist friend Sister Santussika said I'd be welcome at her Theravada monastery. But she encouraged me not to run from my life but to embrace it, and that after I did the work she advised, we would revisit my request. She added that it was okay to admit there were parts of my life with Nils that I didn't miss—and that if I looked at our relationship squarely, it was much more than a fairy tale. Real-life marriages are rich in complexity; they can't be reduced to two-dimensional stories. In fact, neither can fairy tales.

It takes effort and honesty to meet the many challenges that arise in relationships. All relationships are complex, and ours had some particular twists and turns because of our different nationalities and customs. While I was embracing a new country and new languages,

Nils was becoming an active and present papa. Because I tend to be optimistic, having to acknowledge that not every minute of life with Nils was bliss was transformational for me. It gave me the space to let in the truth, including that Nils was an addict and kept things from me. Acknowledging that someone who has died was not perfect can be hard. We want to speak kindly of the deceased. Nils was a wonderful, funny person, a terrific father, a loving husband, and a caring and loyal friend, but at times he tried my patience. Part of healing one's heart is looking objectively at one's relationship and admitting things were not as perfect as we'd wished. There were moments I felt betrayed by him, and at the same time felt the need to protect his reputation. Once I admitted these things, I was able to look honestly at my own life and to trust others again.

Regardless of my passion for sobriety, I had to admit that I was not able to offer it to him. Nils told me every day, "I love you more today than yesterday," yet that turned out not to be enough for him not to harm himself. I had lost faith in humanity, and in some of my husband's words and behaviors. So it was challenging to let trust in. I wasn't interested in loving someone totally and completely again and then having them disappear. Meeting Nils was one of the highlights of my life. Words seem inadequate to express it. But the more I was able to step back from our relationship and see it in full view, I could see that if he had lived, we would have had to improve our communications and he would have had to make his sobriety a priority.

All the effort I invested in my well-being—letting go of Nils, outcomes, and past struggles—put me squarely on a journey of self-discovery and, eventually, self-love. Nils's life *and death* forced me to grow exponentially. Loving myself deeply allowed me to discover love with another all over again. My heart was open the day I watched Craig walk into the meditation room. I was able to recognize his beautiful soul, and I surprised myself that I was willing to commit to someone truly dedicated to his own sobriety and spirituality one day at a time. I had to see those things in myself first before I could recognize them in someone else, again. At the end of each hot yoga practice, participants say *Namaste*, which means "the light in me is a reflection of the light I see in you." We're all mirroring back each other's love, light, and truth.

When we met, Craig and I were each on our own spiritual journey. Then, as our relationship progressed, our journeys began to entwine. Now we love and celebrate a lot of the same things, and at the same time, each of us is independent, following our own path. Craig teases me that I like to trail him, follow him around. On some level that's probably true, because I love playing tennis, swimming laps, working out, scuba diving, traveling, playing golf, and spending time in spiritual places. We are both deeply committed to our sobriety, to making a difference in the world, and to the truth. We don't sugarcoat things, and we have the difficult conversations that are necessary in a relationship. Over the years, Craig has helped me explore what spirituality really means.

Some people think that to show how much you loved someone who has died, you must remain in perpetual mourning—that the amount you grieve is equal to the love you shared. The heart has an infinite capacity to love. We have enough space within to love our parents, our children, our friends, strangers, and, yes, our partners. Parents who have more than one child love each of them uniquely. We can love the person who has died with fervor and devotion, and still love the person we're with now. Love is not a possession. It's not all or nothing. It's not comparison. *Love just is.* It's our true nature and who we are as individuals. When we remove everything else—our material selves, our issues, our challenges, our pain—what remains is infinite love.

To move on and love someone else doesn't take away from or diminish the love you once shared with someone else. I was fortunate to meet Craig, who understands this. He is gracious, generous, funny, sometimes patient, and a bit challenging at times. He's a Leo through and through. According to astrology, Leos have tremendous faith and lay everything at the feet of the gods. Craig understands my need to grieve (it still arises at unexpected moments) and my need to remember. The memories will always be there. Craig helps me look at the past and the present with a certain amount of dry humor. Humor gives us some degree of detachment. When I feel as if I'm in the middle of a hurricane, I step back and envision everyone involved as though we're in a *Saturday Night Live* sketch, and doing so usually helps put things in perspective. It can make the unbearable bearable, and I highly recommend it. We learn valuable lessons through laughing with others, especially when we're able to laugh at ourselves.

My relationship with Craig is multidimensional. It's honest, sometimes challenging, and wonderful. We make each other better people. He shows me what it's like to be present and to have faith. He has a wonderful relationship with his dad, who I adore; and I have wonderful relationships with my parents, who he adores. We travel together and love spending time in spiritual places, whether churches, temples, or the sea, to name a few. We laugh together, do our best to live life fully with passion, and are committed to putting our sobriety first. We also honor that I love getting things done promptly, and he takes his time. We accept our differences. We love ourselves and the world with its infinite wonders. And we take it one day at a time.

Love is possible after loss, but it starts from within. I had to do a lot of inner work to get to a place where I was vulnerable enough to trust another person with my heart. Part of this comes from faith. I know I'm being protected. Rumi says that our assignment in life is not to seek love but to remove the obstacles we've built against it. We must surrender fully to the Divine, which is Love. If it's possible for me, I believe it's possible for anyone.

CHAPTER 11

Five Practices That Help Me Sparkle Like a Sapphire in the Sun: Generosity, Gratitude, Prayer, Meditation, and Ritual

In my defenselessness, my safety lies.
— A COURSE IN MIRACLES

In the years since Nils's suicide, this quote from *A Course in Miracles* has helped me. I feel peaceful and empowered when I embrace my defenselessness. Doing so helps me connect with a deeper wisdom and trust in my higher power, and it respects that Nils and God know what transpired on that fateful day and one day I will know, too. When I take responsibility in this way, I become wiser in my words, deeds, and choices. I get to "be myself" rather than trying to be someone else's version of myself. Instead of remaining bitter, jaded, or closed, I choose, over and over, peace, forgiveness, laughter, and love—which are the portals to generosity, gratitude, and prayer. When the heart bursts wide open, it's energizing and pleasurable to dance in this space.

In Nils, I witnessed acts of generosity that still inspire me. Whenever I go out for a meal or a coffee and see a servicemember, police officer, or firefighter, I always buy their meal or coffee. It makes the person feel good, and it makes me feel good, too. And every time I act spontaneously like this, I'm honoring Nils's spirit and memory. Random acts of kindness are great for the soul.

When I see someone in need, I do my best to help. On a recent trip to India, I saw a mother with two daughters looking at shoes at a local shoe store. They didn't look destitute, but I could see it would be a sacrifice for the mother to buy her daughters shoes. So I purchased them and a few sparkly barrettes before their mom was able to say anything. The joy on the girls' faces carrying their bags with brand-new shoes was priceless. And for me an act of generosity, no matter how small, always sows a seed and is invigorating.

On that same trip to India, I saw a young man buying souvenirs for his family in a spiritual gift shop. He was looking at price tags and being extremely judicious in his purchases. He clearly had lots of gifts to buy. While the man shopped, I went up to the cashier and told him that Craig and I would pay for his entire purchase. When the young man was finally ready to check out, he seemed suspicious of me—a foreign stranger standing next to him interested in what he was buying, until the cashier explained. Without saying a word, the man began to weep, overwhelmed with gratitude and appreciation. I began to cry too, because he was so touched, and felt delighted I could be a part of someone else's happiness. I could feel Nils there too.

Being generous means different things to different people. For me, it means to give freely and abundantly to another soul without wanting anything in return. If you have money to give, then give it if it feels right. Give what you do have—time, energy, a shoulder to cry on. Calling a family member to see how they're doing counts. Listening to a friend is an act of generosity. Participating in your favorite charity. Picking up litter on the street or letting someone take a parking space that you really want or giving a handbag you love to a friend: these are all generous acts. I've given many of my girlfriends some of my beautiful handbags, and it brings me a lot of joy. Anytime you put someone else's needs before your own, you're acting with a generous heart. It's important for our mental health, I believe, to give generously.

Gratitude is energizing, too. I begin and end each day on my knees in gratitude to my higher power, this beautiful energy that exists in all living and nonliving things. This energy has been manifested in Neem Karoli Baba, who was considered a holy man, Mother Earth, and deities like Hanuman, Ganesh, Lakshmi, Narasimha, Krishna, the Buddha, and Jesus. I seek guidance from them, for they are all a part of the cosmic energy that is the life force that exists everywhere. Today I describe and experience my higher power as cosmic energy. This is how I know that I have always been well taken care of by the universe. Feeling grateful in your whole being and expressing it out loud by saying *thank you* throughout the day elevates the soul. It cleanses and renews. By being grateful for all the things I have in my life, for my challenges, and for what has been removed keeps my mind and heart present and attuned. In celebrating the fullness of my life today, I look back on my experiences with Nils with gratitude, laughter, and serenity. So much of what I have today is because of his contribution in my life. The wisdom I've gained over the past two decades is because of what I experienced both loving and mourning him. My heart is full.

I'm abundantly blessed by my relationship with Craig, wonderful friendships, family, sports, community, sobriety, and spirit. All of it has been cumulative, and all of it sprouts from a place of profound sorrow and brokenness. C. S. Lewis said, "The pain I feel now is the happiness I had before. That's the deal." And the inverse is true as well: The happiness I feel now is part of the pain I had before. By staying present with, and growing through the pain, I have been able to come out the other side to happiness. It's possible to be happy and love your life after grief. I know, and I want others to know it, too. It's an inside job, and it doesn't happen overnight. For those still in the thick of acute grief, finding moments to be grateful may seem impossible. So, start small, find the smallest things to be grateful for—the briefest moments of joy: *I'm grateful for my sense of humor. I am grateful for my determination. I am grateful for my willingness. I am grateful that I love to learn.* Nothing is too small to be thankful for, and little by little, they add up. Gratitude helps us take stock of what we *do* have. When we're suffering, it's easy to focus on what we've lost or don't have. But when we live in gratitude, we train our brain to see what we do have. The more attuned we are to all the wealth we have inside us and around us, the more abundant and whole we begin to feel and the more vibrant life becomes.

In addition to generosity and gratitude, prayer has been an essential part of my healing practice. I pray daily for world peace and the happiness of all living beings. Each day, I listen to prayerful music like Krishna Das's chanting and continue to have spiritual experiences while listening to Baba Hanuman, the Hare Krishna chant, and many others. With roots in the Vedic tradition, *kirtan* is a call-and-response chant set to music, expressing loving devotion to a deity. It's often a mantra, such as the name of Ram, one of the Hindu deities, which means God.

Listening to these chants quiets my mind, opens my heart, and makes me feel centered, invigorated, connected, and strong, knowing that all is well, and I'm protected, safe, and loved. I've even taken up playing the harmonium, a tabletop-sized organ with bellows at the back that are pumped by one hand while the other hand plays the keyboard, and I'm learning to play music that honors spirit, my higher power, to name a few, and the universe. I also love listening to Lauren Diagle, who is a Christian singer. I'm attracted to music that honors life and encourages the listener. Playing or listening to spiritual music always brings me closer to myself, to Nils, and to the world, and often brings tears of joy, gratitude, and a deep knowing that I'm right where I'm supposed to be.

Another way I stay connected to Nils is by listening to his favorite music. He loved discovering new bands and downloading their music on his iPhone and iPod. Shortly after his death, I found his iPod with lots of his favorite music and began listening to it as a way to stay close to him. Now whenever I hear Flogging Molly, Coldplay, or Pink, especially her song "Sober" (which was Nils's ringtone for me), it puts a smile on my face. For me, listening to music is a transcendent, transportive experience, a form of prayer.

Nils also felt that movies can be a form of creative prayer because they evoke so many emotions and are a portal to understanding ourselves, resolving issues through the characters, and eliciting emotions that bring us closer to God (as he understood God). He especially loved zombie and action movies, and documentaries, which helped him decompress from stress and connect with humanity. To him, zombies represented the evil in the world and action heroes represented our superpowers in the face of adversity. "Some people pray to relieve stress," he said, "or to be reminded of their strengths. I just watch something I'm interested in and get a similar benefit." He loved being transported in time, if only for half an hour. At night, he watched a *Walking Dead* episode or a documentary, especially films about World War II, before going to bed. He never tired of watching programs about World War II. I asked him why, and he said that it was an important time in human evolution, and it must be remembered for generations to come. I felt his answer was incomplete, but I didn't know what follow-up question to ask.

A year after Nils died, I wanted to honor the anniversary of his passing in Israel, to celebrate his life in a sacred and holy country. I spent several days in Jerusalem at the Wailing Wall praying for him and leaving notes to God in the wall's cracks. This wall represents the troubles of the world. It was incredible to observe those who were drawn there by their faith and those who were simply curious.

While in Jerusalem, I also visited the Yad Vashem World Center for Holocaust Research and Education, *knowing* I would feel Nils's presence. While walking through this structurally beautiful space filled with horrific yet inspirational stories and artifacts, I sat on a concrete bench in a dark room watching and reading quotes from Holocaust survivors. In that moment, I am confident that Nils was sitting on the bench with me, holding my hand and smiling, and it became clear to me why Nils felt so strongly that World War II was important. He'd had a soul connection to the Jewish people and identified with their struggle, sense of powerlessness, and fighting spirit that led them to rebuild even after such a tragedy. I left the museum with a deeper understanding of and appreciation for my late husband, and for the Jewish people's enormous fortitude, and I felt compassion for all involved. This trip to Israel brought me some closure, a sense of community, and a strong reminder of how magnificent it is to be alive.

My appreciation of different cultures' views of spirituality continues to support all aspects of my life—my work, service, travel, and even hobbies. Meditation is an integral part of my life. Being in silence is consistently restorative for me, and practicing meditative silence for extended periods of time provides the spaciousness to *stay present with myself*. I always benefit, regardless of how long I meditate.

After returning to the US, I had the good fortune of becoming friends with Jerry Jones, a spiritual seeker who shared with me his passion for SoHum meditation, a simple practice that uses breath and the repetition of these two syllables to achieve joy and tranquility. Breathe in through your nose and say the syllable *So* silently, and exhale through the nose and say the sound *Hum* to yourself. When breath and awareness come together, they become light. Meditating regularly can lead to the union of the individual with cosmic consciousness, beyond time, space, and thought, beyond cause and effect. I often play Valencia Porter's "Guided So Hum Mediation for Inner Peace" on my iPhone or laptop, and I just love reaping the benefits.

Sitting in meditation, I've learned to give my thoughts the freedom to flow without identifying them. Many of our thoughts are random chatter that lacks usefulness or trustworthiness. When I'm not in alignment with "what is," I feel anxious or uncomfortable. The most effective way for me to release this feeling is to close my eyes, take a few deep breaths, and do a few minutes of SoHum meditation, creating a sense of space in my body, mind, and soul. I move from feeling constricted to being relaxed in just a few minutes. It's quite extraordinary; my body becomes lighter.

When I allow my mind to tell stories, which may be exaggerations about an experience, it's often not useful and doesn't serve me or those involved in the story. Observing your thoughts takes practice, but it's an essential skill. Thoughts and words are powerful. Thoughts can be dangerous or inaccurate or harmful. We have a choice in what we think and believe. We don't have to believe that we're awful or that we should die or that there's no way out. This is the ego talking, the mind doing its thing. We can learn to question our thoughts. The truth is, we are loved. We are all one with the universe.

Death is an illusion. Our bodies die, but our spirits and the love we experience transcend these bodies from lifetime to lifetime. Wherever I am, I know that I am one with Nils and with everyone in the world. And when I'm sitting quietly or in meditation, I become acutely aware of it. It's easy, in our day-to-day lives, to get distracted from the truth of oneness. Meditation quiets us and help us see these truths of our being. It provides the spaciousness we need to relax, settle in, and be open to the infinitude of possibilities. When Craig meditates, on occasion he sees Nils, Baba, and his own mother who passed away years ago, all of them together.

Acts of generosity, expressing gratitude, praying, meditating, and loving my life have become rituals for me. Healing is not linear, like going out and buying a handbag. It's more like riding on a roller coaster. I cherish my life by respecting my sobriety and living an abundant life, which is primarily a state of being, and honoring all the goodness in my life. I love going to morning meetings where we talk candidly, celebrate spirit, express gratitude, pray, and help newcomers. I have incorporated other rituals into my life, too, that help me heal and honor Nils and the life we shared.

On May 8 of each year, the day I found him, I send beautiful photos of Nils to Pierre, Craig, my parents, and a few friends, and ask them to pray for Nils and the kids. I also post a few photos of him on Instagram celebrating his life. Together we honor him and remember. I listen to "Beam Me Up" by Pink, a beautiful song about longing to be with someone who has left this earth but whose soul remains in a parallel universe. Pink sings about how she can feel him with her and yet how she longs to see his beautiful blue eyes and hold his face in her hands. It's as though she wrote those lyrics for me. They put a smile on my face, and I always say out loud, "Love you more today than yesterday." While I still have some sad moments remembering him, I mostly do some fun and creative things to honor him.

On our wedding anniversary, I go on a hike and talk with him. The people I pass must think I'm crazy, because I speak as though he's right next to me. On his birthday, I always watch his favorite movie, *Resident Evil*, an action sci-fi film starring the beautiful Milla Jovovich, who Nils adored. He thought she was a talented actress, loved how she slayed the zombies in the *Resident Evil* series, and considered her the most beautiful woman on the planet. I also spend a few moments praying for him and for my dear friend Terry, who died on Nils's birthday a few years back. They didn't know each other on earth, but I feel confident they know each other now. I feel grateful I pulled off a surprise birthday party for Nils's forty-ninth birthday and flew his parents in for the weekend. Our friend Tim hosted it, and all of Nils's closest friends in Geneva were there. Keeping the secret was challenging, but when his birthday arrived Nils had no clue.

His parents were in on the surprise, and they asked Nils to take them to this little restaurant across Lake Geneva in France. Nils had his favorite spots to eat, so persuading him to travel more than ten miles for dinner was quite a feat. But they succeeded, and we all got in the car and headed toward France. I was chatting with his mom and encouraging him to chat with his dad, doing our best to distract him. He wondered why we were pulling up in front of Tim's house, and I said I'd left something there I needed to pick up. I casually tugged his mom's hand and walked her toward the front door, saying "I'm excited for you to meet Nils's friend."

Nils was getting cranky in the car and finally suggested to his dad that they go inside for a quick minute as well. The front door burst open, and everyone shouted, "Surprise! Happy Birthday!" and tears streamed down his cheeks. He was so touched by the outpouring of love that he grabbed my hand and looked at me as though he were a little boy, his eyes the size of silver dollars, with a ginormous grin. I will cherish moments like these the rest of my life. Whenever Nils grinned, his blue eyes seemed to get even bluer. The whole night he kept whispering into my ear, "I can't believe all these people showed up for me." I just smiled and said, "You are precious and loved by so many." I was in the process of putting together a wonderful fiftieth birthday party, but that never came to pass, so it warms my soul that he had this wonderful experience.

Rituals can be fun, creative, and unique. They can recall the lighter and happier moments with our loved ones. By carving out a time and space for remembering, we honor our beloved and we also free ourselves to *sparkle like a sapphire in the sun*. We can find joy, laughter, purpose, and happiness again. We can live the lives our loved ones would want us to live.

CHAPTER 12

It's All Grace

To give space to All of the forces of the universe. To recognize them all, to allow
them to be, to not try to shove anything under the rug. It's all Grace:
sickness, fatigue, pleasure, pain, there's nothing left in my life other
than the teachings that bring me into union with the Divine.
— RAM DASS

I f someone had told me that one of the keys to recovery would be to give myself some space, I would have thought they were misinformed. What does spaciousness have to do with grief? And what is spaciousness anyway? Let alone a *spacious heart*? And how in the world will a spacious heart transform me?

I've been fortunate to have great spiritual guides, mentors, and teachers who have guided me through life's challenges and celebrations. I've relied on their counsel through phone calls, one-on-ones, group meetings, books, retreats, podcasts, audiobooks, and lectures to help me make sense of my life, and in the process, my compassion and empathy for others have grown. All this effort has made me more aware of the need to *create space* for myself and others. Spaciousness means having room to move, to be, to explore, and to express oneself; and through giving myself the space to be like a child on a playground—sometimes messy, sometimes creative, sometimes unpredictable, and sometimes cooperative—which created the vulnerability and insights needed to transform. Giving those around me the same wonderful spaciousness was equally important for their own growth and our interactions.

Being spacious and staying sober throughout this journey, which have been critical to my recovery, have been essential in keeping my heart open and aware of the immensity of all the exquisiteness around me and in the world. Our attachments, being critical of ourselves and others, and actively participating in addictions are the source of much of our suffering. I knew instinctively I wasn't going to be Humpty Dumpty, that I could be put back together. With time, space, and effort, I would heal and eventually thrive.

Healing from trauma can transform us—into powerful, free, and enlightened beings. Trauma does not have to end in devastation and bitterness, reliving our trauma over and over. By *embracing grief*, allowing it to do its transformational work, and then releasing it (instead of dwelling on it indefinitely), I have discovered new possibilities for my life.

Pema Chödrön says we have to become "intimate" with our feelings. We can't avoid them. We need to see them and face them. But it's a balancing act. If we focus too much on anything, we get trapped. When we zero our focus in on our grief and only our grief, we see nothing else. Similarly, if all we do is focus on our "freedom," we can stay caught in the *idea* of being free and overlook the many other dimensions of the complex beings that we are.

Buddhists and Christian teachings both suggest that we wear *everything* as a "loose garment," an image for being in the flow of life. When I wear loose-fitting clothes, I feel less constricted and more ease and comfort. Practicing detachment (nonconstriction) helps us free ourselves from suffering. When we focus widely instead of narrowly, with some distance and some neutrality, we begin to see new possibilities. We learn to hold the balance between clinging and detaching, intimacy, and autonomy, the past and the present moment. We learn to feel pleasure along with pain, joy along with sorrow, peace along with war, and doing so, we begin to see light in the darkness. Doing so, I have learned to hold the grief, trauma, hope, and beauty in the palms of my hands.

And, most importantly, I've come to see clearly that Love is the answer to everything and the spacious heart that contains that Love is indeed my true home, where I reside, where Nils resides, and where all of humanity resides, too. I trust and know this, and I want you to know it too: *Although you may be struggling mentally, physically, and spiritually now, you can be transformed.* Not just with time—but with *space*—a space that includes loving kindness, awareness, compassion, laughter, forgiveness, gratitude, and trust in a higher power, a power greater than yourself.

My intention in writing this book has been to offer hope to those who have lost a loved one to suicide, to those who have lost a loved one to addiction, to those who are considering suicide, and to those struggling with addiction. Writing it has helped me become whole and gain perspective on my own journey, illuminating what has been the most important thing in my life—my dance with my beloved higher power. My quest has helped me understand that my higher power is playful, loving, supportive, beautiful, giving, creative, and kind. Being in sacred places, spending time with spiritual beings, and having this renewed relationship with my higher power have helped heal many aspects of my life. I have discovered strengths I never knew I had.

Craig and I have a beautiful prayer room filled with marble and wooden *murtis* of Hanuman, Ganesh, Durga, Gandhi, Krishna, the Buddha, Jesus, and Mother Teresa, to name a few. It's important to have a sacred space in your home that is both tranquil and uplifting. Every day is a new opportunity to practice empathy, self-love, forgiveness, mindfulness, patience, and seeing the world with a sense of humor, and I now know that Grace is with me always, in everything.

Nils was more than my best friend. He was and still is one of my greatest teachers. Our journey together, and apart, has elevated my commitment to my sobriety, my relationships with others, making a difference in the world, and living with passion. My gorgeous wedding bands are symbols of our everlasting love, which I will cherish the rest of my life. Like so many people with addictions, Nils thought he had things under control. He was confident there would be no ramifications from his relapse because he wasn't using very often or very much. He underestimated his addiction and paid the ultimate price—his life—and his actions created an enormous amount of pain for those he loved and who loved him. To think that on my birthday on April 22, 2011, just eighteen days before he died, Nils surprised me by playing the song "How Deep Is Your Love" by the Bee Gees. He grabbed my hand, pulled me close to him, gently placed his cheek against mine, whispered in my ear, "I love you, Mrs. Nilsson," and we danced slowly in the kitchen. This was my best birthday yet, because he finally slow-danced with me and gave me his thirty-day sobriety coin. When we take our sobriety and mental health for granted, we risk not only our own lives but also the lives of others.

*   *   *

The difficulty with suicide is no one on the outside ever really knows what is going on in another's mind. And it is a staggering statistic that those whose family members commit suicide are 3.5 times as likely to attempt suicide themselves.[6] More than 50 percent of suicides have some relation to alcohol or drug use—this figure is even higher among adolescents—and up to 25 percent of suicides are committed by drug addicts and alcoholics. It has been recommended that drug addicts or alcoholics undergo evaluation for suicidal thoughts due to their high risk of suicide.[7] Suicide is the tenth leading cause of death in the United States and one of the leading causes of death worldwide, per the World Health Organization. WHO estimates that worldwide every forty seconds someone dies of suicide. It is a global phenomenon in all regions of the world, with the suicide rate increasing, and the strongest risk factor for suicide is a previous attempt.

In addition, the suicide rate among servicemen and -women in the United States is as high as twenty per day, making up 15 percent of total

---

[6] Ping Qin, "The Relationship of Suicide Risk to Family History of Suicide and Psychiatric Disorders," *Psychiatric Times* 20, no. 13 (December 1, 2003), https://www.psychiatrictimes.com/view/relationship-suicide-risk-family-history-suicide-and-psychiatric-disorders.

[7] Maurizio Pompili et al., "Suicidal Behavior and Alcohol Abuse," *International Journal of Environmental Research and Public Health* 7, no. 4 (April 2010): 1392–431, https://www.ncbi.nlm.nih.gov/pmc/articles/PMC2872355/.

suicides. The Department of Veterans Affairs says this estimate includes active-duty troops, guardsmen, reservists, and veterans. Posttraumatic stress disorder may be a leading cause, along with underlying mental health issues, substance abuse, and unaddressed chronic health conditions stemming from service.

If you're reading this book and are at risk in any of these ways, chances are that you're striving desperately to get help and heal. You may be doing everything in your power to find a light in the darkness. All I can say is: *Keep going.* Do things you enjoy that take your mind off your thoughts. *Keep reaching* out to those you trust. We are only a phone call away, an email away, an Instagram chat away. *Keep talking* about your dark thoughts *and* your desire to get better and be healthy. Keep living— one minute at a time, one step at a time, and one day at a time.

The spiritual journey I took to heal was not chronological and was far from traditional. It was messy at times. Each person's journey through grief and loss is different. What I've attempted to show is that if I could do it, it's possible for you. We're all on a journey in this life, and our paths may be similar or extremely different. This is what makes life a great adventure.

Being open to the possibility that you are filled with Grace and that you're surrounded by Grace will make the journey a bit easier, but I understand this may not be where you're starting. I certainly wasn't ready to accept that Grace was present in the early days of my journey. Grace reveals itself in the little miracles—in the *aha!* moments, in the sunrise, and so much more. It just *is.* Right after Nils's suicide, I wrestled with my spiritual convictions. Having doubts is perfectly natural. Bring them along with you on your path of discovery toward healing.

Another thing I did along the way was to face my fears, both real and imagined, and to reach out for help. It's okay to be afraid. It's natural. There's nothing wrong with you. Talk about the things that scare you, become intimate with them, and break through. Let others take your hand and assuage your anxieties. I love the vision of Dorothy, the Tin Man, the Scarecrow, and the Cowardly Lion in *The Wizard of Oz,* who banded together to weather whatever came up while walking the yellow brick road together to see the Wizard. When they finally met the Wizard, they realized that all along, they had what they were seeking inside of them—the Tin Man had a heart, the Cowardly Lion had courage, the Scarecrow had a brain, and Dorothy was home wherever she was. Much like the characters in *The Wizard of Oz*, I felt my entire world falling apart; but in the wake of destruction, a new life emerged. It was impossible to believe at first, but looking back on the past thirteen years, I can say with confidence that indeed, life has a way of rebuilding itself when we allow it to.

There were moments I blamed others and even sought revenge. If I had indulged any of these impulses for too long, my life would be vastly different. I would have stayed both mentally and physically ill, not to mention behind bars. *Mental health affects our whole body.* Many of us suffer physical pain and even disease, because we haven't healed the brokenness inside us. Taking care of our bodies, eating healthily, moving, building social connections, serving others, and letting go of old habits and self-destructive behaviors are all vital to improving our mental, spiritual, and physical health.

I healed because I was vulnerable, flexible, adventurous and willing to live consciously and practice compassion, empathy, and forgiveness. I was fortunate to be part of a support group from the beginning, a wonderful network of friends who were there to help me. Sometimes it takes effort to find these resources, sometimes they appear at our doorstep, but they are available to everyone.

I had the help I needed to maintain and nurture my sobriety, take full responsibility for my behavior, and enjoy my life. The fellowship has a slogan: "We absolutely insist on enjoying life." To better honor my continued gift of sobriety, I widened my focus to include celebrating life and approaching life with lightness of being. When I moved back to the States, I was folded into the Breakfast Club, six or so members who have breakfast together after a regular morning meeting. We often make light of our lives. We laugh about past choices and past consequences. It's critical at times to step back and see the Cosmic Giggle in some of our life choices and experiences.

Most communities have support groups for suicide survivors, for those who have lost loved ones to addiction, for those struggling with suicidal ideation and substance addiction. Support groups abound through churches, spiritual centers, and even online. And if you are struggling with an addiction of any kind, there are plenty of resources by phone and online, where people will help you and love you through your crisis. I share some of them at the end of this book.

Becoming more spacious and willing to thrive opened up astonishing possibilities. The universe had its hand in my serendipitous meeting with Craig. There are thousands of weekly meetings in the Los Angeles area. It was by Grace that Craig and I attended the same meeting at the same time and met. He, too, is a bright light. It's extraordinary how similar Nils and Craig are. They both have big bubbly personalities and a fervor for life. They would have been the best of friends, talking endlessly about travel, sports, VIP upgrades, their Starwood-Marriott Ambassador Elite benefits, and so much more. In actuality, they are the best of friends since the soul is eternal.

It's true that my life is very different today. I'm a widow. I no longer live in a big house, fly in private jets, live in Europe, listen to my step kids talk about their day, and hear multiple languages spoken at home. My life is much simpler, but it's still bountiful, with new hobbies, different work, and gorgeous moments like going to Gilbert's with my mom for chips and salsa, spending time with Craig's dad at assisted living, swapping stories with a girlfriend about our boyfriends' behavior, going to Hamburger Habit with my dad for lunch, strolling through Bloomingdale's (my favorite store), and attending the BNP tennis tournament with friends, to name a few. The richness in my life is a direct result of the extraordinary people I'm surrounded by and saying yes to growing and having new experiences. Moving from Europe forced me to take a leap of faith that everything, indeed, was *falling together*. It can be challenging to move on when you're surrounded by memories. And for some, of course, staying in place can be the healing balm you need. Trust that you'll know what's best for you. Sit in stillness and the answers will come, sometimes in words, sometimes in a vision, sometimes in a feeling.

Through generosity, gratitude, prayer, meditation, and ritual, my life is sparkling again. If you take away anything from this book, it's that *you can survive a suicide and flourish.* You will experience joy again. You will laugh again. You will love again. Some people may feel it's necessary to honor their loved one by grieving endlessly. That's probably the last thing your loved one would want you to do.

In September 2022, more than ten years after Nils died, a dear friend sent me a clipping from *Expressen,* one of Sweden's two national evening newspapers, dated May 11, 2011:

> *Businessman Nils Nilsson made hundreds of millions from IT shares on the Stockholm Stock Exchange. He invested his fortune in Russia and brought with him investors such as tennis great Stefan Edberg, financier Robert Weil, Swedish pensioners, and the storied Dinkelspiel family. This weekend Nils Nilsson died unexpectedly in Switzerland and his death has spread shock in the Swedish business community. Next week Nils Nilsson was to gather the shareholders of the real estate company Ruric for a general meeting at Strand Hotel at Nybrokajen in Stockholm. He was the company's centerpiece as founder and could offer the good news that Ruric has been profitable. But instead, it will be a day of mourning when the shareholders gather at Nybrokajen on Sunday—horrific and incredibly tragic. "Nisse was in many ways a genius, a super entrepreneur who always had a thousand ideas about what to do next," colleague Tom Dinkelspiel told* Dagens Industri *[a Stockholm-based financial newspaper].*

I knew Nils was a successful businessman, but until reading this more than a decade after he died, I'd had no idea how high the stakes of his ventures were. It took grit and belief in himself to accomplish what he did professionally. Getting sober also takes an enormous amount of grit and perseverance. His story clearly conveys that getting sober and taking care of one's mental health are not contingent on material success. This is not a business deal that one can negotiate the terms of. The article also expresses vividly how quickly things can change. What touched me the most was that he would be missed, was respected, and was loved.

The greatest expression of love you can show someone who has died is by living an incredible life in their honor. Love your life and, as Tony Robbins encourages, "Live with passion." Climb mountains. Swim in the ocean. Feel the warm sand between your toes. Let raindrops sprinkle on your face. Take in the sweet smell of roses. Taste and savor the cappuccino in a bustling café, or whatever it is that you love. Dance to your favorite songs. Sing till your voice hurts. Laugh until your stomach hurts. Hold the hand of a stranger or a loved one. Comfort a sick or grieving friend. Pay for someone's meal or coffee. Surprise someone with a gift. Tell someone that you love them and are proud of them. Hold space for them to open up to you. *Live. Live. Live.* Love. Love. Love. Sparkle like a sapphire in the sun. And while you're living and loving this life and flourishing in it, know that your loved ones are smiling. They are happy. They are free. And so are you. For this freedom resides at home in the space in your heart—forever and always. It has been there the whole time. As Neem Karoli Baba said, "The heart never grows old. See only God. Love Everyone." It's all Grace.

You are here to enable the divine purpose of the universe to unfold.

That is how important you are!

— ECKHART TOLLE

Mental Health
and Addiction Resources

According to recent data, someone in the United States commits suicide every eleven minutes. This alarming rate translates to approximately 49,476 deaths by suicide in 2022, as reported by the National Institute of Mental Health (NIMH). This statistic highlights the severity of the issue, emphasizing the need for comprehensive suicide prevention strategies and resources.

If you are struggling with mental health issues and/or addiction issues, there are lots of great resources worthy of reaching out to for information and support. Please see the links below.

DEPRESSION RESOURCES

Depression and Bipolar Support Alliance, https://www.dbsalliance.org

Families for Depression Awareness, https://www.familyaware.org

Mental Health America, https://www.mhanational.org

Substance Abuse and Mental Health Services Administration
(SAMHSA), https://www.samhsa.gov

WebMD Depression Health Center, https://www.webmd.com/depression

GRIEF RESOURCES

Association for Death Education and Counseling (ADEC),
    https://www.adec.org

Family Caregiver Alliance: National Center on Caregiving,
    https://www.caregiver.org

Hospice Foundation of America, https://hospicefoundation.org

Living Dying Project, https://www.livingdying.org

Lots of Helping Hands, https://lotsahelpinghands.com

National Adult Day Services Association, https://www.nadsa.org

National Alliance for Caregivers, https://www.caregiving.org

National Family Caregivers Association (NFCA),
    https://caregiveraction.org

Visiting Nurse Associations of America, https://www.vnaa.org

Well Spouse Association, https://wellspouse.org

SUICIDE PREVENTION HOTLINES

988 Suicide and Crisis Lifeline, 800-273-8255,
  https://suicidepreventionlifeline.org

The Samaritans, 800-870-4673, https://samaritanshope.org

Veterans Crisis Line, 988, press 1, https://www.veteranscrisisline.net

SUICIDE PREVENTION RESOURCES

American Association of Suicidology, https://suicidology.org

American Foundation for Suicide Prevention, https://afsp.org

National Council for Suicide Prevention, https://www.thencsp.org

National Institute of Mental Health, https://www.nimh.nih.gov

National Organization for People of Color Against Suicide,
  http://nopcas.org

Suicide Awareness Voices of Education (SAVE), https://save.org

Suicide Prevention Awareness and Support, www.suicide.org

Suicide Prevention Resource Center, https://www.sprc.org

THE TWELVE STEPS
AND ADDICTION RESOURCES

Alcoholics Anonymous (AA), https://www.aa.org

Cocaine Anonymous (CA), https://ca.org

Narcotics Anonymous (NA), https://www.na.org

Recovery Connection, https://www.recoveryconnection.com

Substance Abuse and Mental Health Services Administration (SAM-HSA), https://findtreatment.gov

Workaholics Anonymous (WA), https://workaholics-anonymous.org

Resources I Highly Recommend

Babin, Leif, and Jocko Willink. *Extreme Ownership: U.S. Navy Seals Lead and Win.* New York: St. Martin's Press, 2017.

Dyer, Wayne. *The Power of Intention: Learning to Co-create Your World Your Way.* Carlsbad, CA: Hay House, 2004. Audio CD.

Goldstein, Joseph. *Mindfulness, A Practical Guide to Awakening.* Louisville, CO: Sounds True, 2016.

Hawking, Stephen. *A Brief History of Time.* UK: Bantam Books, 1989.

Hawkins, David. *The Discovery: Revealing the Presence of God in Your Life.* Wheeling, IL; Nightingale Conant, 2011. Audio CD.

———. *Peace Is the Natural State.* Sedona, AZ: Veritas Publishing, 2003. Audio CD.

Hicks, Ester, and Jerry Hicks. *The Law of Attraction: The Basic Teachings of Abraham by Ester Hicks.* Carlsbad, CA: Hay House, 2006. Audiobook.

Kornfield, Jack. *The Art of Forgiveness, Lovingkindness, and Peace.* New York: Bantam Books, 2002.

Lama, Dalai & Tutu, Desmond. *The Book of Joy.* New York, Penguin Random House, 2016.

Madones, Cloe. *Behind the One Way Mirror* Zeig, Tucker & Theisen Inc. Publishers, 2019.

McRaven, Admiral William H. *The Hero Code: Lessons Learned from Lives Well Lived.* New York: Grand Central Publishing, 2021.

Pema Chödrön. *Don't Bite the Hook: Finding Freedom from Anger, Resentment, and Other Destructive Emotions.* Boston: Shambhala Publications, 2007. Audiobook.

Porter, Valencia. "Guided So Hum Meditation for Inner Peace." 2023. Video, 18:48. https://www.youtube.com/watch?v=A8EZjJQs38I.

Purja, Nims. Beyond Possible. Washington D.C.: National Geographic, 2022.

Ram Dass. *Cultivating a Compassionate Heart.* Louisville, CO: Sounds True, 2000. Audio CD.

———. *Polishing the Mirror: How to Live from Your Spiritual Heart.* Louisville, CO: Sounds True, 2014. Audiobook.

Robbins, Tony. *Personal Power.* El Segundo, CA: Guthy-Renker, 1996. Audio CD.

Tolle, Eckhart. *A Life of Inner Peace.* Novato, CA: New World Library, 2004. Audio CD.

———. *The Art of Presence.* Louisville, CO: Sounds True, 2007. Audio CD.

———. *The Power of Now.* Canada: Namaste Publishing, 1997.

Wolfelt, Alan. *The Wilderness of Grief: Finding Your Way.* Fort Collins, CO: Companion Press, 2010.

✳   ✳   ✳

If you need help or support, please reach out.
I would love to hear from you.
Contact me, Kimberly Nilsson, PsyD,
through my website,
https://www.kimberlynilsson.com

Acknowledgments

My friend John was the first to encourage me to write as a way to heal and make sense of my experience. As my writings were transformed into a book, he was the driving force. John was always generous with his time, funny, and loved playing the guitar. He wrote a fabulous song about a frog, which he sang often. It uplifted the heavier moments, for which I will always be grateful.

As the book developed, I had a lot of help. Thank you to my friends Mary and Arnie, who helped me continue exploring this life-transforming process of writing. Mary shares my enthusiasm for beautiful handbags, and Arnie shares my love for Hawaii. My thanks to Karen for her skillful and thorough copyediting, Mark for his precise proofreading, Lisa for her creative ease designing this book, and the team at Epigraph Books for encouraging me to publish my experiences about a subject that can be uncomfortable for many.

Thanks to my dad for crying with me when I felt sad and for smiling with me when I felt happy. His unconditional love and support helped me muddle through some very dark moments until I was able to embrace more beautiful moments.

Thanks to my mom for worrying about me and for loving me as though I were only a child. Her ability to express her love for Nils while loving me helped me heal.

Thanks to my brother for being honest with me in the early days after Nils's death. He dared to share his outrage at Nils's action but also had deep compassion for him.

Thanks to my nieces and nephews for reminding me to maintain a childlike way of being.

Thanks to the Wizard of Oz, Daryl, for being strong, determined, and focused, and for reminding me to stay calm and know that everything would ultimately be fine.

Thanks to Jack and Raushana for their unconditional love, humor, and grace, and their availability to talk to me through whatever was going on.

Thanks to Pierre for his feisty and sensitive spirit and for loving Nils. He kept a close eye on me and loved me like a sister.

Thanks to my sponsor Debbie in Geneva for her spiritual guidance and overall down-to-earth way of being. She held my hand, gently guided me through what seemed to be a mountain of messes, encouraged me to experience the vast array of feelings that arose, and reminded me that everything was "falling together."

Thanks to my friend Vegas for encouraging me to strengthen my *Ichinen* (determination) by chanting, for Skyping with me at a moment's notice, and for reminding me that I have my grandmother's resilience.

Thanks to Freddie for inspiring me one step at a time while on Mont Blanc and for helping me maintain high standards while enjoying the journey.

Thanks to the Breakfast Club members for getting together after the 12-step meetings. You helped me see my past with some humor and my present with even more humor.

Thanks to my sponsor Cynthia for walking through the doors of the meditation center with an open heart and for sharing her love and faith in the 12-step program, the Hindu gods, and the *bhakti* movement.

Thanks to the 12-step programs and its members for changing the trajectory of my life.

Thanks to my many teachers and their teachings: Baba, Tony Robbins, Pema Chödrön, Esther Hicks, Wayne Dyer, Ram Dass, Jack Kornfield, the Dali Lama, Trudy Goodman, Dr. David Hawkins, Cloe Madanes, Jesus, *The Secret*, Deepak Chopra, Eckhart Tolle, for reminding me of who I am, what I am capable of, where to put my focus, and what is really important in life. You have been my gurus and have guided me through all that living entails.

Thanks to Craig for sharing his love of sports, travel, and laughter, but most importantly for his love of Ram (God). His dedication to deepening his relationship with the Beloved is contagious. Our serendipitous meeting breathed light into my life.

Thanks to the Krishna Center for their gorgeous *Aarti's* in the wee hours of the morning and for warmly welcoming me into their beautiful space to worship and heal.

Thanks to Mother India for always being there for me, for folding me into the exquisite beauty of this holy land.

Thanks to the sea for always welcoming me and sharing its gorgeous and invigorating beauty.

Thanks to my step kids for being incredible teachers.

Thanks to Dr. Yvan Gasche for caring for Nils those three days he was in the ICU at the hospital in Geneva, for his willingness, compassion, time, and love in helping me come to terms with Nils's death and the importance of my continuing to live my life fully.

Thanks to the unknown man who helped me get Nils down from the rafter and for performing CPR on him until the ambulance arrived. His courage and willingness to help me, a complete stranger, through the most horrific moments of my life will always be remembered.

About the Author

KIMBERLY NILSSON has a doctorate in clinical psychology, has worked as an Addiction Recovery Specialist for more than a decade. She is certified as a Grief and Trauma Specialist and has been involved in the 12-step fellowship more than thirty years. Kimberly continues to do volunteer work for a variety of organizations. When she met the love of her life, Nils, she changed nearly everything and moved to Switzerland to be with him. After a whirlwind romance, they married at a simple ceremony in New York's Central Park.

In 2011, her seemingly fairytale life ended abruptly when she came home to find her beloved husband hanging in the carport. To survive the shocking way Nils had ended his own—and their—life together, Kimberly had to gather all her inner strength, rely on her training, deepen her evolving spiritual practices, and educate herself about suicide and its ramifications for those left behind; and eventually to flourish. Though no longer in the field professionally, she continues to help others stay sober and cultivate a meaningful life by speaking openly about addiction, mental health, and suicide prevention.

Made in the USA
Las Vegas, NV
26 January 2025

17006284R00111